A-LEVEL YEAR 2

STUDENT GUIDE

AQA

Psychology

Issues and debates in psychology

Options: relationships, stress and aggression

Molly Marshall

PHILIP ALLAN FOR
HODDER
EDUCATION
AN HACHETTE UK COMPANY

Philip Allan, an imprint of Hodder Education, an Hachette UK company, Blenheim Court, George Street, Banbury, Oxfordshire OX16 5BH

Orders

Bookpoint Ltd, 130 Park Drive, Milton Park, Abingdon, Oxfordshire OX14 4SB

tel: 01235 827827

fax: 01235 400401

e-mail: education@bookpoint.co.uk

Lines are open 9.00 a.m.–5.00 p.m., Monday to Saturday, with a 24-hour message answering service. You can also order through the Hodder Education website: www.hoddereducation. co.uk

© Molly Marshall 2016

ISBN 978-1-4718-5679-2

First printed 2016

Impression number 5 4 3 2 1

Year 2020 2019 2018 2017 2016

This Guide has been written specifically to support students preparing for the AQA A-level psychology examinations. The content has been neither approved nor endorsed by AQA and remains the sole responsibility of the author.

Typeset by Integra Software Services Pvt. Ltd., Pondicherry, India

Cover photo: Shutter81/Fotolia

Printed in Italy

Hachette UK's policy is to use papers that are natural, renewable and recyclable products and made from wood grown in sustainable forests. The logging and manufacturing processes are expected to conform to the environmental regulations of the country of origin.

Contents

Content Guidance

Questions & Answers

■ Getting the most from this book

Exam-style questions

Commentary on the questions

Tips on what you need to do to gain full marks, indicated by the icon **e**

Sample student answers

Practise the questions, then look at the student answers that follow.

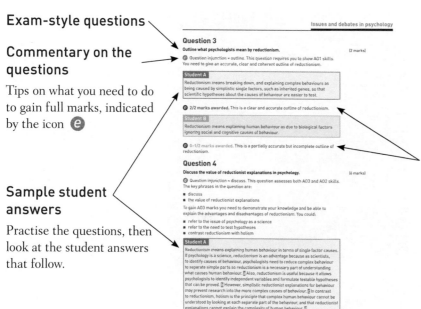

Commentary on sample student answers

Find out how many marks each answer would be awarded in the exam and then read the comments (preceded by the icon **e**) following each student answer. Annotations that link back to points made in the student answers show exactly how and where marks are gained or lost.

■About this book

This is a guide to **issues and debates in psychology and options in psychology (relationships, stress and aggression)** which are examined on A-level Paper 3. The guide is intended as a revision aid rather than as a textbook or revision guide.

For each of the topics in this guide — issues and debates in psychology, relationships, stress and aggression — the following are provided:

■ appropriate content relevant to each topic. This is not intended as the *only* appropriate content for a given topic, but gives you an idea of what you might include and how you might present an answer to a question on a particular aspect of the specification

■ a glossary of key terms, constructed to be succinct but informative

■ example questions in the style of AQA A-level examination questions, together with full explanations of their requirements as well as the appropriate breakdown of marks between AO1, AO2 and AO3 skills

■ an example of an A-grade response to each of these questions, showing how the question might be answered by a strong student

■ an example of a C/D-grade response to each of these questions, with comments showing where marks have been gained or lost

How to use this guide

This guide is not intended to provide a set of model answers to possible examination questions, or an account of the right material to include in any examination question. It is intended to give you an idea of how your examination will be structured and how you might improve your examination performance.

You should read through the relevant topic in the Content Guidance section before you attempt a question from the Questions & Answers section. Look at the sample answers only after you have tackled the question yourself.

Content Guidance

This section gives content guidance on issues and debates in psychology and options in psychology. The options included are relationships, stress and aggression.

Each topic contains information on the theories and studies that comprise the specification content. Knowledge of appropriate theories, studies and research methods is essential for the examination. It is also important to be able to assess the value of these theories, studies and research methods.

At the end of each topic a glossary of key terms is provided — those terms that you will need to use, or may be asked to define, in an examination. Author names and publication dates have been given when referring to research studies. The full references for these studies should be available in textbooks should you wish to read about or research the topic further.

■ Issues and debates in psychology

Gender and culture in psychology: universality and bias

Cultural bias

Culture can be defined as 'the beliefs, attitudes, social and child-rearing practices etc.' that people of a group share and that distinguishes one group from other groups. You need to understand the issues of ethnocentrism and cultural relativism.

Ethnocentrism

Ethnocentrism is the effect that your own cultural perspective has on the way you perceive other cultures and people from other cultures. Most research is carried out by Western (Europe and USA) organisations and it is often assumed that what is true of our culture is also true of other cultures. For example, the concept of 'self' evolved in the English language at the time of the Industrial Revolution and is associated with a view of a person as an individual. However, many cultures view the person within his or her social or family context and the self-concept is less distinctive. Many studies of personality in non-Western cultures have been assessed using translated personality tests, rather than devising new, culture-relevant tests.

Emic or etic

Emic constructs are traits that are specific to a certain culture (e.g. monogamy in Western culture). Etic constructs are universal traits that can be found across cultures (e.g. family). Berry (1969) suggests that in the history of psychology, emic (culturally specific) constructs have been assumed to be etic. For example, in the

> **Knowledge check 1**
>
> Explain what is meant by ethnocentrism.

study of intelligence in Western culture, intelligence has been defined as problem solving, reasoning and memory and these constructs have been used to measure intelligence in other cultures. However, these measures might not be relevant in other cultures. For example, the skill of hunting which was essential for survival in preliterate society may not be relevant to intelligent behaviour today. Other emic constructs could include research into conformity, relationships and diagnosing psychological disorders.

Cultures differ as to whether they are **individualistic** or **collectivist**. In individualistic cultures, one's own identity is defined by personal characteristics and achievements, independence and self-identity. In collectivist cultures, identity is defined by collective achievements and interdependence.

Cultural relativism

Cultural relativism is the view that beliefs, customs and ethics are relative to the individual within his or her own social context. In other words, right and wrong are culture-specific — what is considered moral in one society may be considered immoral in another. Since no universal standard of morality exists, no one has the right to judge another society's customs. Cultural relativists avoid ethnocentrism by the belief that all cultures are worthy in their own right and are of equal value.

One of the main problems with the idea of defining behaviour as normal or not is that none of the definitions copes with cultural variation. Cultural relativists suggest that beliefs about abnormality differ between cultures and that behaviour seen as normal in one culture may be seen as abnormal in another.

In Western culture:
- physical and psychological components of a disorder are separate and emotional aspects are seen as important
- mental illness can be caused by psychological conditions and may be treated by psychological processes
- the individual has a 'self' which is experienced as continuous over time, is distinct and unique

However, there are cultural variations in the way people experience psychological disorders. For instance, non-Western cultures do not always consider emotional experience as separate from bodily experience and so patients may complain of physical ailments rather than psychological distress. Some cultures treat religiously induced trance-like states as acceptable spiritual experiences, while other cultures see the same behaviour as a symptom of mental illness. For example, an American Indian who hears the voice of a recently deceased relative calling from the after-world would consider this to be a normal experience, whereas a British person may see this as a hallucination.

Bias in psychological research

Temporal bias. All cultures change over time. For example, in the 1950s British culture was very different from today, e.g. homosexuality was seen as a mental illness.

Research and sample bias. Smith and Bond suggest that bias arises because of the way research is carried out. Problems may arise because of translation, and also because, although in cross-cultural research, samples may be taken from

Knowledge check 2

When considering the characteristics of different cultures what is the difference between emic or etic constructs?

Exam tip

You could be asked to explain what is meant by cultural relativism.

similar groups (e.g. students), the social backgrounds and life experiences of the participants from different cultures may be very different. For example, a student in England will have had a very different upbringing, compared to a student in China or Africa. Sears (1985) found that 82% of psychology studies used undergraduates as participants (51% used psychology undergraduates). This means that most research conclusions are based on samples of middle-class, academic, young adults (most often male) who are not representative of Western cultures or of global populations.

Gender bias

Alpha and beta bias

When considering gender and culture in psychology, other types of bias that occur are **alpha** and **beta bias**.

- **Alpha bias.** When alpha bias occurs, research tends to emphasise and over exaggerate differences between cultures (or between genders). Differences are exaggerated in order to suggest that one culture (usually Western) or one gender (usually male) is superior to others. Examples include Ainsworth's strange situation and research by Yerkes (1917) into intelligence.
- **Beta bias.** When beta bias occurs, research tends to minimise or ignore differences between cultures (and genders). Any theory based on research conducted with one cultural group, that is then presented as a theory of all human behaviour is beta biased. Examples of research where beta bias is argued are Kohlberg's theory of universal stages of moral development, Freud's psychodynamic theory of personality development, evolutionary theories of behaviour where men are portrayed as hunting and women looking after children and Asch's research into conformity.

The effect of ethnocentrism and alpha and/or beta bias is to create and perpetuate stereotypes and to make cultures (and genders) seem more different (or more similar) than they are. For gender bias, you might consider research that suggests males as aggressive but females nurturing, males as skilled at spatial orientation but females better at verbal skills, or males as being independent but females as dependent.

Androcentrism

Androcentrism occurs when male views and behaviour are viewed as 'the norm' and used to explain both male and female behaviour. Androcentrism also occurs when female behaviour is different from male behaviour and is construed as abnormal or inferior because it is different. For example, Kohlberg's theory of moral development is androcentric. He based his initial research on male samples and he assumed that moral thinking was similar between the sexes. He then conducted studies comparing male and female moral development and suggested that while the majority of males operated at level 4, most females operated at level 3. Other examples of androcentric psychology are Bowlby's research into attachment and maternal care that suggested women should stay at home and care for children, Freud suggesting that women suffered from 'penis envy' and Erickson's proposal that women were destined to bear and care for children.

Knowledge check 3

When undertaking research into gender what is the difference between alpha bias and beta bias?

Exam tip

Make sure you can give an example of research that is alpha or beta biased and explain why.

Free will and determinism

Most people feel that they have free will to make choices and that their behaviour is not determined for them but is the product of their own volition. However, this position creates difficulties for scientific research which assumes causal and deterministic relationships. Determinism suggests that individuals cannot be held responsible for their actions.

- **Hard determinism** suggests behaviour is caused by genetic factors.
- Some psychologists see the source of determinism as being outside the individual, a position known as **environmental determinism**. For example, Bandura (1961) showed that children with violent parents will in turn become violent parents through observation and imitation.
- The term **soft determinism** is often used to describe situations in which people do have a choice, but their behaviour is subject to some form of biological or environmental pressure.
- **Psychic determinism** suggests all mental processes are determined by the unconscious or pre-existing mental complexes. For example, the assumption made by Freud that childhood experiences during the development of the ego and superego will shape all future thought processes.

The psychological approaches

Physiological approach (hard determinism). This approach usually sees behaviour as being caused by some biological factor. If this is the case then behaviour is determined by biology, thus the individual has no free will to choose to behave differently.

Cognitive approach (free will). This approach explains behaviour as being caused by cognitive factors (e.g. thought processes, attention, decision making). Thus it does allow free will to choose behaviour. For example, in cognitive behavioural therapy, it is assumed that the person can choose not to think irrationally. However, some cognitive psychologists explain behaviour as being caused by maturation (ageing) in which case behaviour is determined by biology, thus the individual has no free will to choose to behave differently. For example, Piaget suggests that children's thought processes change at predetermined ages, thus giving a deterministic explanation.

Humanistic approach (free will). The humanistic approach assumes that people have free will and that behaviour is not determined. Humanistic psychologists believe that in the exercise of free will people have 'personal agency' and that we can make choices in life, the paths we go down and their consequences.

Social approach (soft determinism). This approach looks at the behaviour of people in groups and whether the research allows 'free will' may depend on which approach is used. For example, Milgram maintained that although his participants were influenced by the social situation they were in, they had the free will to choose not to continue giving electric shocks.

Learning approaches (environmental determinism). These usually explain behaviour in terms of stimulus-response learning caused by past experience. If this is the case then the individual does not have the free will to choose to behave differently because behaviour is determined by past experiences.

Exam tip

To help you revise, draw up a table showing the approaches and whether 'generally' they give deterministic explanations for behaviour or whether they allow free will.

Psychodynamic approach (psychic determinism). This approach explains behaviour in terms of unconscious forces which the individual can neither escape nor explain. In addition, because the unconscious forces are the result of early childhood experience, behaviour is determined by two factors — the past and unconscious motivation — so individuals have no free will to choose their behaviour.

The nature-nurture debate

To what extent is any behaviour the result of your genetic code (nature — the genes you inherit) or your life experiences (nurture — your parents, your upbringing, your experiences generally)? This debate is especially relevant in the areas of language, aggression, gender and dysfunctional behaviour. Some research explains behaviour as being caused by nature (ageing) — for example, Piaget suggests that children's thought processes change at predetermined ages. Other research, for example, Bandura, demonstrates that behaviour is not innate, and that children who observe adult role models behaving aggressively learn from what they see and imitate aggressive actions.

These days, few psychologists take the extreme nature or extreme nurture approach. Many researchers take an **interactionist approach** looking at the extent to which both biology and the environment influence behaviour. However, it is not possible to disentangle the effect of multiple genetic factors from the effect of environmental factors such as social experience and culture. For example, a child may be genetically programmed to be a tall basketball player, but if he never receives healthy food or exercise then that potential may go unrealised. These days, many researchers are interested in seeing how genes modulate environmental influences and vice versa.

The psychological approaches

Physiological approach. Some research suggests that behaviour is caused by biological factors and if this is the case then behaviour is caused by nature. However, research by Maguire found that the hippocampi in the brains of taxi drivers changed as a result of their environment which suggests an interaction between nature and nurture.

Cognitive approach. An example of the nature-nurture debate in cognitive psychology is the question of how children acquire the ability to use human language. On the nature side of the argument is Noam Chomsky who proposes that we are born with an innate, biological, language acquisition device which facilitates, during a critical period, the development of language. On the nurture side of the argument are the behaviourists, especially Skinner, who propose that we learn to use human language by imitation and reinforcement — but many attempts to teach non-human primates to communicate using human language have not given a definite answer to this question.

Social approach. Much social research takes the nurture side of the debate, showing that behaviour is influenced by the social environment. For example, research by Piliavin et al. demonstrated that it was not the dispositional characteristics of the passengers, e.g. their kind nature, but the situation of the victim, lame or drunk, which influenced whether help was given.

> **Knowledge check 4**
>
> Explain the difference between biological determinism and environmental determinism.

Learning approaches. These explain behaviour in terms of nurture. From the perspective of behaviourists, when we are born we are a 'blank slate' and from the moment of birth we learn our behaviour.

Psychodynamic approach. This perspective recognises the influence of both nature and nurture. According to Freud, the id is the innate (nature) part of the human personality driving us to seek pleasure and avoid pain, but the ego and superego are developed as a result of early experiences (nurture).

Holism and reductionism

Levels of explanation for behaviour

Behaviour can be explained in terms of the following four levels:

- The **biological level** of explanation focuses on the biological and chemical processes underlying behaviour. For example, a biological level of explanation for aggression might focus on the role played by genes or hormones or activity in specific brain areas.
- The **basic processes** level of explanation focuses on the psychological (e.g. cognitive) processes that are universal across humans. For example, a basic processes level of explanation for aggression might focus on the thoughts and emotions that precede it.
- The **person level** of explanation focuses on individual differences in behaviour. For example, a person level of explanation for aggression might focus on personality differences in people.
- The **sociocultural level** of explanation focuses on the influence of other people on behaviour by studying behaviour in social and cultural contexts. For example, a sociocultural level of explanation for aggression might focus on how being in a crowd influences whether people behave aggressively.

Reductionism

Reductionism is the principle of analysing complex things into simple constituents or the use of simple principles, for example explaining complex human behaviour in terms of simplistic single factor causes, such as inherited genes. One of the basic goals of science is to reduce all phenomena to separate simple parts to understand how they work, so reductionism may be a necessary part of understanding what causes human behaviour. Reductionist hypotheses are easier to test and the fact that they can be 'proven' (or not) makes them more believable. However, reductionist explanations distract psychologists because simplistic explanations for behaviour may prevent further attempts to find more complex but less clear-cut explanations.

Holism

Holism is the principle that complex phenomena cannot be understood through an analysis of the constituent parts alone because the behaviour of the 'whole system' cannot be explained in terms of the 'sum' of the behaviour of all of the different parts. Reductionism is a goal of science, but although simple explanations are appropriate in some situations, simple explanations rarely explain the richness of human experience and prevent the search for more complex answers.

Exam tip

Make sure you can write an argument, giving examples, explaining whether each approach to psychology suggests behaviour is caused by nature or nurture.

Knowledge check 5

Identify the four levels of explanation used in psychology.

Exam tip

Remember that many psychological explanations which are reductionist are also deterministic.

The psychological approaches

Physiological approach. Physiological (biological) reductionism explains behaviour in terms of biological factors, especially when explaining behaviour in terms of genes, as in some explanations of dysfunctional behaviour.

Cognitive approach. This can be described as reductionist when it proposes a computer-like information processing approach as a means to describe and explain behaviour.

Learning approaches. These use a very reductionist vocabulary: stimulus, response, reinforcement and punishment. This is called **environmental reductionism** because behaviourists reduce the concept of the mind to behavioural components, i.e. stimulus-response links.

Psychodynamic approach. This is reductionist because it relies on the interaction between three components, the id, ego and superego, to explain complex behaviour.

Exam tip

Make sure you can explain what is meant by reductionism and give an example of reductionist research.

Idiographic and nomothetic approaches

- The term **nomothetic** comes from the Greek word 'nomos' meaning 'law'. Psychologists who take a nomothetic approach to psychological investigation study groups to make generalisations about behaviour.
- The term **idiographic** comes from the Greek word 'idios' meaning 'own'. Psychologists who take an idiographic approach to psychological investigation want to discover what makes each of us unique.

The difference between the nomothetic and idiographic approaches influences the research methods preferred by psychologists:

- Experimental and other quantitative methods are favoured from a nomothetic point of view.
- Case studies, informal interviews, unstructured observation and other qualitative methods are idiographic.

Nomothetic examples include: classification manuals like the DSM-IV which classifies people according to particular types of disorders; behaviourist experiments with animals (e.g. rats, cats and pigeons) to establish laws of learning (B. F. Skinner); Milgram used the nomothetic approach to draw general conclusions about obedience.

Idiographic examples include Freud and the case study method (e.g. Little Hans) where patients are interviewed over a long period of time and qualitative records are kept of his interpretations.

Behaviourist, cognitive and biological approaches tend to take a nomothetic approach and focus on establishing generalisations. Humanistic approaches are interested in the individual and are thus idiographic.

The psychodynamic approach is arguably idiographic, because although Freud suggests that the structure of the unconscious mind (id, ego, superego) is common to everyone, each patient's individual problems (e.g. Hans' phobia) arise from unique childhood experience.

The nomothetic approach

■ Experimental, quantitative research enables prediction and control of behaviour, and objective, controlled methods allow for replication, generalisation and the development of general laws of behaviour.

■ However, when we make predictions about behaviour from a small group the results may ignore individual differences and/or may only give a limited understanding of what motivates behaviour.

The idiographic approach

■ Qualitative research provides a more complete (holistic) understanding of an individual's behaviour.

■ However, findings from qualitative methods such as case studies cannot be generalised to a wider population and such methods are subjective, unstructured and unscientific.

Knowledge check 6

Cognitive psychologists who carry out experimental research into eyewitness memory conclude that memories are reconstructions. Explain whether this research is nomothetic or idiographic.

....

Ethical implications of research and theory

The *Oxford English Dictionary Online* (2007) defines ethical behaviour as being 'in accordance with the principles of ethics; morally right; honourable; virtuous; decent', and it defines ethics as 'the whole field of moral science'. For psychologists, core ethical principles are relevant to research with human participants.

Ethics in research

Ethical issues may arise because of a conflict of interest between the researcher and the researched. The researcher may wish to collect in-depth high quality data from those most closely affected by whatever is being researched. The risk is that the researcher may be tempted to consider unethical research practice in order to try to obtain the data. For example, participants in Milgram's research were placed in a very stressful situation, and in the 'arousal stage' Bandura deliberately caused distress to young children.

Ethical risks and responsibilities

Researchers are responsible for causing something to happen in relation to the lives of research participants, and need to consider the potential physical or psychological risks and how they will take responsibility for addressing these potential risks. The researcher is responsible for ensuring that the level of risk is minimised and that participants are fully aware of any risks before they agree, freely, to participate.

The risks may be physical or psychological arising from the discussion of sensitive topics, stirring painful memories or the disclosure of personal information. Ethical issues relate especially to interview methods, where participants may be encouraged to disclose personal information, but there are ethical judgements to be made in all research involving human participants.

The following research would normally be considered as involving more than minimal risk:

■ research involving vulnerable groups, such as children aged 16 and under, those lacking capacity or individuals in a dependent or unequal relationship

- research involving sensitive topics such as participants' sexual behaviour, their legal behaviour, their experience of violence, their gender or ethnic status
- research involving access to records of personal or confidential information
- research involving access to potentially sensitive data through third parties such as employee data
- research that could cause psychological stress, anxiety or humiliation
- research involving invasive interventions such as the administration of drugs
- research that may have an adverse impact on employment or social standing
- research that may lead to 'labelling' either by the researcher or by the participant
- research that involves the collection of human tissue, blood or other biological samples

Basic principles of ethical research

Informed consent. There should be informed consent from participants before they take part. This means that people should know exactly what they are being asked to do, and what the risks are, before they agree to take part. A participant will normally be asked to sign a **consent form** to record informed agreement to take part.

No pressure on individuals to participate. Incentives to take part should generally not be provided. If an incentive is used it needs to be only a token, and not enough to encourage someone to participate who would really prefer not to take part.

Respect individual autonomy. Autonomy means the freedom to decide what to do. Even when someone has given consent to participate they must be made aware that they are free to withdraw from the study at any time, without giving a reason. They must also be able to request that the data they have given be removed from the study.

Avoid causing harm. The duty of the researcher is not to cause harm and judgements need to be made about what are acceptable levels of harm.

Maintain anonymity and confidentiality. Making data 'anonymous' means removing the contributor's name. However, researchers need to take more than this basic step to protect a participant's identity. Other information can help to identify people, for example job title, age, gender, length of service, and the more pieces of information that are presented together, the easier it is to identify someone. 'Confidentiality' relates to the protection of the data collected. Where the aim of your research is specifically to access private feelings, stories and concerns, you will need to be clear about how the confidentiality of that data will be respected.

Research with vulnerable groups. Care is needed in research with young children, and with people who are ill, or recently bereaved. However, others may be vulnerable in certain contexts, for example students, employees, dependents or people with particular traits that could be subject to prejudice.

Socially sensitive research. There is increasing research interest in 'sensitive' social issues such as sexuality, child abuse and death, domestic violence, partner abuse and family breakdown. The aim has been to gain increased understanding and awareness of the impact of the experience of 'sensitive' issues on people's lives. The sensitive nature of the research may not be apparent at the beginning of the research project. Alternatively, a subject that was presumed to be of a sensitive nature may not be.

Knowledge check 7

List three examples of research topics that might involve some risk to participants.

Exam tip

You must be able to describe and apply the basic principles of ethical research.

Research is likely to be sensitive when:

- it intrudes into some deeply personal experience
- the study is concerned with deviance or social control
- the study investigates the vested interests of powerful persons or the exercise of coercion or domination
- it deals with things that are sacred to those being studied

Any topic could potentially be seen to be sensitive depending on the people being researched and their feelings about the topic may also arise when in-depth interviews and detailed questionnaires are used that may unleash painful emotions and memories in participants.

Exam tip

Be prepared to give an example of research that could be categorised as 'socially sensitive'.

Issues and debates in psychology: glossary of terms

alpha bias: research tends to emphasise and over exaggerate differences between cultures (or between genders).

androcentrism: male views and behaviour are viewed as 'the norm' and used to explain both male and female behaviour.

beta bias: research tends to minimise or ignore differences between cultures (and genders).

cultural relativism: the view that beliefs, customs and ethics are relative to the individual within his or her own social context. Cultural relativists believe that all cultures are of equal value.

culture: 'the beliefs, attitudes, social and child-rearing practices etc.' that people of a group share and that distinguishes one group from other groups.

determinism: the assumption that people cannot be held responsible for their actions because their behaviour is determined (caused) by factors outside their control.

emic/etic: emic constructs are traits that are specific to a certain culture; etic constructs are universal.

environmental determinism: the assumption that behaviour is caused by factors outside the individual, e.g. classical conditioning.

ethnocentrism: the effect that your own cultural perspective has on the way you perceive other cultures and people from other cultures.

free will: the assumption that people have the free will to select and decide their own behaviour.

hard (biological) determinism: biological explanations suggest behaviour is caused by genetic factors.

holism: the principle that complex phenomena cannot be understood through an analysis of the constituent parts alone, because the behaviour of the 'whole system' cannot be explained in terms of the 'sum' of the behaviour of all of the different parts.

idiographic: comes from the Greek word 'idios' meaning 'own'. Psychologists who take an idiographic approach to psychological investigation want to discover what makes each of us unique.

individualistic/collectivist culture: in individualistic cultures, one's own identity is defined by personal characteristics and achievements, independence and self-identity; in collectivist cultures, identity is defined by collective achievements and interdependence.

levels of explanation for behaviour: psychologists use four levels of explanation for behaviour — biological processes, basic psychological processes, the attributes of the person enacting the behaviour and sociocultural processes.

nature or nurture: nature — the extent to which behaviour is the result of genes, biology, hormones, age, gender; nurture — the extent to which behaviour is due to life experiences such as parents or upbringing or culture.

nomothetic: comes from the Greek word 'nomos' meaning 'law'. Psychologists who take a nomothetic approach to psychological investigation study groups to make generalisations about behaviour.

psychic determinism: the type of determinism that suggests all mental processes are determined by the unconscious or pre-existing mental complexes.

reductionism: the principle of breaking behaviour into simple constituents or the use of simple principles, for example explaining complex human behaviour in terms of simplistic single factor causes, such as inherited genes.

sample bias: participants are drawn from one group (e.g. students) and then findings are generalised to explain behaviour from different cultures.

socially sensitive research: research into 'sensitive' social issues such as sexuality, child abuse and death, domestic violence, partner abuse and family breakdown. Research is likely to be sensitive if it investigates very personal experiences.

soft determinism: the theory that in some situations people do have a choice, but their behaviour is subject to some form of biological or environmental pressure.

temporal bias: assuming that findings from previous research done many years ago can be applied to explain behaviour today.

Knowledge summary

You should be able to demonstrate knowledge and understanding of:

- gender and culture in psychology: gender bias, including androcentrism and alpha and beta bias; cultural bias, including ethnocentrism and cultural relativism
- free will and determinism: hard determinism and soft determinism; biological, environmental and psychic determinism. The scientific emphasis on causal explanations
- the nature-nurture debate: the relative importance of heredity and environment in determining behaviour; the interactionist approach
- holism and reductionism: levels of explanation in psychology; biological reductionism and environmental (stimulus-response) reductionism
- idiographic and nomothetic approaches to psychological investigation
- ethical implications of research studies and theory, including reference to social sensitivity

When answering questions on issues and debates in psychology you will be expected to illustrate your answers with knowledge and understanding of research topics studied across the specification.

■ Relationships

Many people spend a great deal of time thinking about their relationships and why they like some people more than they like others. This topic focuses on evolutionary explanations for partner preference, factors affecting attraction, theories of romantic relationships, and virtual and parasocial relationships.

Evolutionary explanations

Research into interpersonal attraction looks at the initial factors that determine why we are attracted to others. Evolutionary psychologists propose that mate choice is unconsciously guided by cues that indicate some survival advantage for offspring, and that because parental investment in reproduction is different for males and females, mate choice cues are different for males and females.

Sexual selection and human reproductive behaviour

Parental investment. Human females invest a great deal of time and energy in their offspring. A baby spends 9 months in the womb and is helpless and dependent on the mother at birth, and requires intensive rearing. As a result, in her lifetime a female has relatively few offspring and requires a mate who is willing and able to provide resources and support for her and her offspring. This theory implies that a female will seek quality in her mate. From the evolutionary perspective women should be attracted to males who have social and economic advantages, who possess valuable resources, and who appear willing to share these resources. On the other hand, male parental investment may be low. A male's reproductive capacity is only limited by the number of females who are willing to reproduce with him, thus males may be more inclined to seek a number of fertile mates. Also, males will want to make sure they are not tricked into raising the offspring of another male. From the evolutionary perspective men should be attracted to females who show signs of good reproductive potential, indicated by physical characteristics such as smooth skin, white teeth, glossy hair, youth and healthiness, and should also seek sexual faithfulness.

Both males and females will be interested in good genetic quality in order that their offspring survive. Some signs of 'good genes' are youth, a healthy complexion, athletic build and symmetry, which may explain why symmetry has been found to be important in perceived attractiveness.

> **Exam tip**
>
> In your revision, summarise the evolutionary explanation to suggest why males and females look for different qualities in romantic partners.

Research evidence

Waynforth and Dunbar (1995) analysed personal adverts in US newspapers. They found that 42% of males wanted younger partners compared to only 25% of females. Also, 44% of males advertised for physically attractive partners but only 22% of females did. Females advertised their attractiveness, but males advertised their economic resources. Buss et al. (1992) found that as measured by galvanic skin response (which assesses autonomic nervous system activity) men showed greater physiological distress than women when asked to imagine scenes of sexual infidelity.

➡

In a cross-cultural study (Cunningham 1986) men were asked to rate photographs of women. Large eyes, small nose and chin, prominent cheek bones, high eyebrows and a big smile were the characteristics most associated with female beauty. Buss proposed that these facial characteristics are associated with 'baby' features, that 'baby' features evoke attraction and caregiving, and that humans have evolved a preference for these facial characteristics to ensure we care for our young. Buss concluded that men all over the world share the same ideal of beauty.

Evaluation

Although Darwin proposed that human mate choices would be guided by the same cues that motivate animal mate choices, human behaviour may be very different from animal behaviour because it is motivated more by cultural and cognitive factors. Also, evolutionary explanations offer an 'after the fact' explanation for behaviours that are continuously observed.

Factors affecting attraction in romantic relationships

Self-disclosure

Self-disclosure is the act of revealing ourselves, consciously or otherwise, to another person. It comprises everything an individual chooses to tell the other person about himself or herself. The information can include thoughts, feelings, aspirations, goals, failures, successes, fears, dreams as well as one's likes and dislikes.

There are two dimensions to self-disclosure — **breadth and depth** — and both are important in developing a fully intimate relationship. The range of topics discussed by two individuals is the breadth of disclosure and the degree to which the information revealed is private or personal is the depth of that disclosure. It is easier for breadth to be expanded first in a relationship because it consists of outer layers of personality and everyday lives, such as occupations and preferences. Depth in disclosure is more difficult because it may include painful memories and traits that we prefer to hide. This is why we reveal ourselves most thoroughly and discuss the widest range of topics with our spouses and close family.

Self-disclosure is an important building block for intimacy and intimacy cannot be achieved without it. We expect self-disclosure to be reciprocal and appropriate. Self-disclosure can be assessed by an analysis of cost and rewards which can be further explained by **social exchange theory** (see page 18). Most self-disclosure occurs early in the development of a relationship, but more intimate self-disclosure occurs later. Sexual self-disclosure is the act of revealing one's sexual preferences to one's sexual partner — this fosters understanding and intimacy. Relationship satisfaction was found to correlate with sexual disclosures, and for men, high levels of sexual self-disclosure predicted higher relationship satisfaction, though this was not true for women. But, sexual satisfaction was linked to higher levels of sexual self-disclosure for both men and women.

Knowledge check 8

What is the difference between breadth of self-disclosure and depth of self-disclosure?

Self-disclosure in marriage. Self-disclosure is a method of relationship maintenance. Partners learn a shared communication system, and disclosures are a large part of building that system. Research suggests that wives' perceptions of their husbands' self-disclosures are a strong predictor of how long a couple will stay together. Those who think their husbands are not sharing enough are likely to break up sooner and those husbands and wives who reported the highest ratings of marital satisfaction showed the highest ratings in intimacy.

Physical attractiveness

Perhaps the first thing we notice about others is what they look like and **physical attractiveness** may be one of the most important factors in interpersonal attraction. Feingold (1992) found that if a person is physically attractive we attribute other positive characteristics, such as sociability, to them as well. This is called the **halo effect** and in the early stages of relationship formation physical attractiveness is an important factor. However, not everyone is equally beautiful. Walster et al. (1966) in the **matching hypothesis** suggested that we are attracted to people whom we perceive to be similarly attractive to ourselves. That we compromise to avoid being rejected by potential partners who are more attractive than ourselves. Physical attractiveness may be an important factor because, from an evolutionary perspective, physical characteristics, such as good skin and glossy hair, indicate breeding success.

Research evidence

The matching hypothesis: Walster, Aronson, Abrams and Rottman (1966)

A group of 664 students were invited to attend a 'computer dance'. They were told they would be 'matched' to a partner by a computer. Before the dance, each student completed a series of questionnaires, supposedly so that the computer could complete the 'matching'. In reality the students, who had been rated for physical attractiveness by the experimenters, were randomly allocated to pairs in which the only control was that the male was taller than the female.

After the dance the students were asked to complete questionnaires on which they rated how much they liked their partner, whether they wanted to see their partner again, how attractive they found their partner and how attractive they thought their partner found them. There was a significant positive correlation between the experimenters' rating of the physical attractiveness of both the male and female students and how much they were liked by their partner. There was also a significant positive correlation between how attractive the students rated their partner and how much they liked them.

Is physical attractiveness an advantage?

Stewart, J. E. (1985) looked for a correlation between the attractiveness of defendants and the severity of punishment awarded. Sixty criminal trials were studied: 56 male and 4 female (27 black, 3 Hispanic and 30 white) defendants were observed by at least two observers and rated on physical attractiveness, neatness, cleanliness and quality of dress which were combined to produce

➜

> **Exam tip**
>
> Check that you can summarise what is meant by self-disclosure.

> **Exam tip**
>
> Make sure you can explain what is meant by the matching hypothesis.

an attractiveness index. Stewart found that defendants who were judged to be less attractive received more severe punishment.

Hunsberger and Cavanagh (1988) found that students rated attractive teachers as nicer and happier than unattractive teachers.

Is physical attraction associated with positive characteristics?

Wheeler and Kim (1997) investigated the **halo effect**. They found that American, Canadian and Korean students rated physically attractive people as more friendly, extrovert, happy and sociable. Landy and Siegall (1974) asked male participants to evaluate an essay to which was attached a picture of either an attractive or unattractive female (the supposed author). Half the participants were given the good essay and half the poor one. The essays (good and poor) were rated as better if they were thought to be written by the attractive author.

Evaluation

- In the computer dance study, a correlational design was used, and it could be that the students rated their partner as more attractive because they liked them, rather than rating their liking based on how attractive they perceived their partner to be.
- Dermer and Thiel (1975) found that very attractive females may be judged as self-centred and materialistic. Sigall and Ostrove (1975) found that female criminals who were perceived to have used their attractiveness during their crime (e.g. fraud) got longer sentences.
- Attractiveness may only be important in the early stages of a relationship. Murstein and Christie (1976) found a correlation between husbands' ratings of how satisfied they were with their marriage and how attractive they thought their wife was and thought them to be. They found no correlation between the wives' satisfaction with their marriage and their perception of their husbands' attractiveness or how attractive their husbands found them.

> **Knowledge check 9**
>
> In the Walster et al. computer dance study how is the sample biased?

> **Exam tip**
>
> You should be able to explain why the Walster et al. computer dance study gives a reductionist explanation for interpersonal attraction.

Filter theory

Kerckoff and Davis (1962) propose a relationship formation theory known as the filter model. They propose that **three filters** are important before we enter a relationship and at different times in a relationship. We start with a field of those who are free for relationships — **the availables** — and gradually narrow them down to a field of those who we would consider as potential partners — **the desirables**.

- The first filter stage is the **social and demographic variables**, where we tend to pick people with a similar educational and economic background to us.
- The second filter stage is the **similarity of attitudes and values**, where people with different values, attitudes and interests from us are filtered out.
- The third filter stage is the **complementarity of emotional needs**, where we decide how well as two people we fit together as a couple.

Research evidence

In support of the social and demographic variables filter, Kandal (1978) asked secondary school students who was their best friend among a group of students and found that best friends tended to be of the same age, religion, sex, social class and ethnic background. Also, in longitudinal research, Kerckoff and Davis tested the filter theory using student couples who had been together for either more than, or less than, 18 months. Over a period of 7 months, the couples completed several questionnaires which gathered data on attitude similarity and personality traits. They found that attitude similarity was the most important factor up to about 18 months into a relationship, but that after this, psychological and emotional compatibility were more important.

Evaluation

The filter model is a useful way to think about factors that influence relationship development and the importance of demographic factors and similarity of attitudes and values in relationships. However, the theory was written in 1962 which means that there is low historical validity (temporal bias) as the research was conducted at a time when Western ideals were dominant. Also, the theory ignores important differences in relationships (imposed etic), for example between cultures or in same-sex couples.

Another criticism is that much research into filter theory is based on biased samples, for example both Kerchkoff and Kandal used all student participants thus their research cannot be generalised to explain factors causing attraction in mature adult relationships.

Theories of romantic relationships

We may like to believe that relationships are formed because of deep feeling and mutual emotional regard between partners, but psychological theories suggest that we form and maintain our relationships mainly because of self-interest. This topic focuses on psychological theories of how romantic relationships are formed and maintained and how they break down.

Social exchange theory: Thibaut and Kelley (1959)

This theory focuses on the interactive nature of relationships. It assumes that relationships are based on 'exchanges' in which each person seeks to maximise their rewards and minimise their costs and thus make a profit. Rewards may include being looked after, companionship and even sex. Costs may include time and effort and financial investment. The model proposes that people stay in relationships when they are 'in profit' but that relationships may fail when either partner's costs exceed their rewards.

This theory proposes **four stages** in the development of a relationship:

Stage 1: sampling stage in which the potential costs and rewards of a new relationship are considered and compared to other known relationships.

Knowledge check 10

List the stages of filter as proposed by Kerckoff and Davis.

Exam tip

Make sure you can evaluate the research into the different factors affecting attraction in romantic relationships (i.e. self-disclosure, physical attractiveness, matching hypothesis and filter theory).

Stage 2: bargaining stage in which partners receive and give rewards to test whether a deeper relationship is worthwhile.

Stage 3: commitment stage in which relationship predictability increases and because each partner knows how to 'get rewards' from the other, costs are reduced.

Stage 4: institutionalisation stage in which norms are developed and patterns of rewards and costs are established for each partner.

The theory also proposes a **comparison level by** which people judge all their relationships. Our personal comparison level is the accumulation of all our relationship experiences. If we judge that the profit from a potential new relationship is greater than our comparison level then the partner will be viewed positively and a new relationship formed. If we judge that the profit from a potential new relationship is less than our comparison level then the partner will be viewed negatively and no new relationship formed.

Knowledge check 11

The social exchange theory proposes four stages in the development of a relationship. Can you outline these four stages?

Research evidence

Profit and loss

Rusbalt and Martz (1995) propose that women stay in abusive relationships because their investment is high (children and somewhere to live) but the cost of leaving is higher (nowhere to live and no money). Thus the woman is still 'in relationship profit' and she will remain in the relationship.

Aronson and Linder (1965) researched four conditions to test the effects of profit and loss on how much a confederate was liked when he evaluated participants.

(1) Positive — all positive evaluations given.

(2) Negative — all negative evaluations given.

(3) Overall profit — negative evaluations followed by positive evaluations.

(4) Overall cost — positive evaluations followed by negative evaluations.

Participants in the overall profit condition liked the confederate more than those in the positive condition, and participants in the overall cost condition disliked the confederate more than those in the negative condition.

Evaluation

- This theory can be applied to different kinds of relationships (e.g. friendships, colleagues, lovers) and, because people will perceive rewards, costs and their comparison level differently, can be used to explain individual differences because what is acceptable for one person may be unacceptable for another.
- The theory proposes that the basis for the formation of human relationships is self-interest and that relationships are based on selfish concerns. Even if it is true, perhaps the model only explains the formation of relationships in individualistic cultures.
- The theory is based on subjective judgement of what constitutes a reward, cost or profit, and thus can be used to justify almost any behaviour in terms of a calculated profit outcome.

- The theory focuses on the perspective of the 'individual in the relationship' and ignores the social world (social context) in which the relationship exists. Families, children, friends, neighbours and shared social events can also be important factors in the formation of relationships.
- Walster et al. (1978) propose that in the development of relationships, fairness in exchange (equity) is more important than the overall amount of profit.

Knowledge check 12

Suggest one reason why it may be difficult to obtain a valid measure of the costs and benefits of a relationship.

Equity theory: Walster et al. (1978)

Equity does not mean equality, it means fairness. The **equity theory** of relationship maintenance assumes that people try to ensure that their ongoing relationships are fair and that people become distressed, and may leave the relationship, if they perceive unfairness:

- People who give a great deal in their relationship but who receive little in return may perceive inequity and become dissatisfied.
- People who receive a great deal but who give little in return may also perceive inequity and become dissatisfied.

This theory predicts that partners should feel equally dissatisfied if they under or over benefit — the greater the inequity, the greater the dissatisfaction and the less likely it is that the relationship will continue. What is considered to be fair is each partner's subjective judgement of their respective inputs and outputs and deciding whether a relationship is equitable may involve complicated calculations.

The theory proposes that an equitable relationship is one in which one partner's benefits divided by their costs is equal to the other partner's benefits divided by their costs. If the result of this calculation results in perceived inequity (unfairness) we may try to restore fairness in one or more of the following ways:

- change the amount we put into the relationship
- change the amount we receive from the relationship
- change our subjective evaluation of relative inputs and outputs to restore the appearance of equity
- compare the relationship with our comparison level for other relationships
- be persuaded by the partner that our subjective perception of relative inputs and outputs is wrong

Research evidence

Hatfield et al. (1979) interviewed newly married couples. They found that under-benefited partners were the least satisfied, over-benefited the next and those who perceived their relationship to be equitable to be most satisfied.

Equity in short-term relationships: Clark (1984)

Male participants were introduced to a female and told that she was either (a) married and visiting the area or (b) single and a newcomer to the area who wanted to make friends.

→

Participants were asked to circle numbers on a sheet after the female confederate had already circled some. Clark predicted that if participants were told the female was married they would circle in a different colour pen (so their input in the circling task would be distinct), but that if the participants were told she was 'single and looking for friends' they would circle in the same colour pen (put more in because they expected to get more out):

- 90% in the married condition chose a different colour pen
- 90% in the single condition chose the same colour pen

Evaluation

Equity theory takes a 'rational economist' approach to explaining human relationships, but in relationships people may be influenced by emotion rather than by rational thought. Perhaps such explanations only apply to short-term relationships in young people in Western culture (emic). Clark and Mills (1979) propose that long-term relationships are maintained because each partner wants to meet the needs of the other. In long-term relationships there is less concern for equity because partners believe things will balance out over time.

It is difficult to see how romantic relationships can be studied in the laboratory, and research studies such as that by Clark (1984) are low in mundane realism. It is also difficult to gain a valid measure of a person's subjective assessment of their inputs to, and benefits from, their relationships as their judgement of these may vary from day to day.

Knowledge check 13

Emic constructs are traits that are specific to a certain culture. Suggest why the equity theory of relationships may be an emic construct.

Exam tip

To help you with your revision, draw up a list of the strengths and limitations of social exchange theory and equity theory.

The investment model (Rusbult 1980)

Commitment is an important factor in maintaining relationships. Rusbult (1980) defined commitment as 'a person's intention to maintain the relationship and to remain psychologically attached to it'. Rusbult's **investment model of commitment** consists of three processes that are positively associated with commitment:

- **Satisfaction level** refers to the positive versus negative emotions experienced in a relationship. A person whose needs are met by his or her partner will enjoy a higher level of satisfaction.
- The **quality of alternatives** is defined as the attractiveness of the best obtainable alternative to a relationship. For example, if someone's need for intimacy could be met elsewhere, their quality of alternatives would be high.
- **Investment size** is how much an individual has already invested in the relationship — where investment can be financial (a house), temporal (time spent together) or emotional (such as in the welfare of the children). A person may stay in a relationship because they have already invested significantly in it.

Rusbult also proposes two other factors linked to commitment:

- **Equity**, the ability to be fair. Rusbult suggests that fairness in a relationship is important because unfairness causes distress, and a partner in an inequitable relationship will be less committed to the relationship and may want to end the relationship.

- **Social support** such as family and friends. If family and friends approve of and support the relationship this produces a positive influence on commitment causing the couple to stay together longer.

Research evidence

Rusbult studied the relationships of students and found that satisfaction and investment were key predictors for staying in the relationship, while availability of alternatives was a trigger for ending the relationship.

Sprecher (1988) carried out a study which supports Rusbult's theory. The aim was to study the extent to which different factors explained commitment to relationships. Data were collected from 197 couples. Relationship commitment was predicted to correlate positively with satisfaction, investment and social support, and correlate negatively with alternative quality and inequity. Results showed that the variables except investment were related (as predicted) to relationship commitment and the two most important predictors of relationship commitment were satisfaction and alternatives.

Evaluation

- As with equity theory, it is difficult to see how human romantic relationships can be studied in the laboratory, and many research studies such as that by Sprecher rely on self-report.
- Since qualitative factors, such as satisfaction with a relationship, may vary from week to week it is difficult to gain a reliable measure of a person's subjective assessment of their investment into their relationship.
- When findings are correlations between factors researchers cannot make statements about cause and effect.
- Much research into relationships is based on the self-report of student samples, and the relationships of young people are usually more volatile than the relationships of older people.

The breakdown of relationships

Duck (1999) proposed three factors to explain why relationships breakdown:

- **Lack of social skills.** Some people lack social and interpersonal skills which leads others to perceive them as uninteresting and disinterested in 'relating to them'. This leads to relationships failing before they really begin.
- **Lack of stimulation.** People expect their relationships to develop and, according to social exchange theory, stimulation is rewarding and lack of it leads to boredom and/or disinterest, which in turn lead the dissatisfied partner to end the relationship.
- **Maintenance difficulties.** As proposed by equity theory, relationships require a lot of input by both partners if they are to be successful. If partners are separated, for instance if one partner is relocated following a job change, and daily contact is decreased it may be difficult for the relationship to survive.

Knowledge check 14

Summarise Rusbult's investment model of commitment to a relationship.

Exam tip

For theories of romantic relationships, make a list of the similarities and differences between social exchange theory, equity theory and the investment model of commitment.

The four-stage model of relationship breakdown (Duck 1999)

Stage 1: intrapsychic phase. There may be little outward show of dissatisfaction with the relationship but one partner may be inwardly re-evaluating the relationship in terms of the costs and benefits. There may be an attempt to put things right, but if this fails, eventually the dissatisfied partner will communicate his or her feelings.

Stage 2: the dyadic phase. The dissatisfied person tells the other partner. This phase is characterised by arguments as to who is responsible for the relationship problem. There may be discussion as to how the relationship can be repaired, but both partners are aware that the relationship may end.

Stage 3: the social phase. Partners have informed friends and family about the problems in the relationship and these others may try to help or may take sides. Friends and family may both speed up the eventual ending of the relationship, perhaps by interfering, and may provide social support when the relationship does end.

Stage 4: the grave dressing phase. Both partners try to justify leaving the relationship and their actions, and construct a representation of the failed relationship that does not present them in unfavourable terms. This process is important because each partner must present themselves to other possible 'future' partners as trustworthy and loyal.

Evaluation

Strengths

The Duck model shows the processes that take place when a relationship fails. Relationship counsellors can use this model to help repair failing relationships. For example, if the relationship is in the dyadic phase, partners can be helped to focus on taking positive steps to repair the relationship rather than focusing on the past and arguing about 'who is to blame'.

Limitations

The model does not explain why relationships break down, it only describes relationship breakdown. The model focuses on what people do rather than how they feel, and emotional satisfaction or dissatisfaction is an important factor when trying to understand why romantic relationships break down.

Virtual relationships in social media

Virtual relationships

Electronically mediated interaction alters the way we communicate with and meet others. It also changes the way in which relationships develop and are maintained. Physical attraction and eye contact is absent and thus what is written (the text) increases in importance. Electronically mediated communication is seen as inferior to face-to-face communication because it offers potential partners reduced information to go on when developing a relationship. This reduction in cues leads to a form of deindividuation in which partners who are more or less anonymous may behave in an uninhibited manner and may breach social norms. However, non-face-to-

Knowledge check 15

Outline the four stages of relationship breakdown as suggested by Duck (1999).

Exam tip

Make sure you can explain the difference between the intrapsychic phase and the dyadic phase of relationship breakdown.

face communication is not new; people have been conducting, and maintaining, relationships by letter and telephone for decades and during the Second World War many women communicated with their partners/husbands for years only by letter.

Advantages and disadvantages of virtual relationships

Electronic relationships have advantages. Duck (1999) reports that those who lack social skills, who live in rural areas, or who have physical handicaps may benefit. Internet chat rooms allow people to make a range of friends they would otherwise not get the opportunity to meet in 'real life'.

Young (1999) proposed the Anonymity, Convenience and Escape (ACE) model of computer-mediated communication, and the Social Identity model of Deindividuation (SIDE) suggests that in computer-mediated communication awareness of individual identity is replaced by awareness of group identity and that being anonymous leads to strong social relationships in groups that meet on the internet.

Perhaps the main disadvantage of electronic relationships is the possibility of deception. Van Gelder (1985) describes a case in which a male psychiatrist who wanted to experience what it was like to be a woman pretended to be a psychologist 'Joan', who had supposedly been injured in a road accident. 'Joan' set up an online support group for other disabled women and over 2 years deceived many women by forming intense friendships and romances. Ling and Helmerson (2002) researched mobile phone use in young people. They found that mobile phones can be used by children to develop and maintain relationships outside the control of parents, and that mobile phones allow young people to develop independence from the family.

Virtual relationships: self-disclosure

The development of a relationship is related to an increase in self-disclosure (see page 18). Being able to disclose the characteristics of one's true self can create bonds of understanding between people and heighten the intimacy of a virtual relationship.

The ability to be **anonymous** in a virtual relationship is important because when anonymous, the costs and risks of social sanctions for what is said or done are reduced. In a face-to-face relationship there is often a cost to disclosing negative aspects of one's self. These barriers are usually not present in virtual relationships and while anonymity can bring out the worst in an individual, it can also allow for the expression of one's true feelings without fear of repercussion. Research suggests that virtual relationships can be characterised as containing high levels of self-disclosure and that people will often reveal themselves far more intimately than they would do in face-to-face relationships.

Research evidence

Parks and Floyd (1996) studied the relationships formed by internet users. They found that people report disclosing significantly more in their virtual relationships compared to their real-life relationships.

In the series of studies reported by Joinson (2001a) self-disclosure was significantly higher in discussions based on Computer Mediated Communication (CMC) compared to Face-to-Face (FtF) discussion. A second

$\rightarrow$

> **Knowledge check 16**
>
> Suggest one reason why individuals might form virtual relationships with those they would not consider to be potential partners in 'real life'.

study compared the level of self-disclosure in FtF discussion, CMC discussion and CMC with video link discussion. In the CMC plus video link the levels of self-disclosure were similar to that in the FtF discussion, but in the CMC with no video link there were significantly higher levels of self-disclosure. These findings suggest that anonymity, especially being visually anonymous, leads to higher levels of self-disclosure.

Exam tip

Make sure you can list two differences between normal relationships and virtual relationships.

Virtual relationships: the absence of gating

Bargh, McKenna and Fitzsimons (2002) looked at how and why relationships that start over the internet are more intimate than those which start in a face-to-face physical communication. They found that some aspects of online virtual communication compared to face-to-face communications enable a deep level of intimacy to form quickly.

When you talk to someone online, you are able to be your **true self** without the usual physical gating features present in face-to-face encounters. Gating features are the physical or material barriers that may arise between people when they interact in person. Physical appearance, age, clothing, race and class distinctions all function as distractions to the expression of one's true self. In virtual relationships, such gating features do not exist.

Knowledge check 17

Explain what is meant by 'the absence of gating in virtual relationships'.

Parasocial relationships

Parasocial relationships are one-sided relationships, where one person extends emotional energy, interest and time, and the other party, the **persona,** is completely unaware of the other's existence. Parasocial relationships are most common with celebrities, organisations (such as sports teams) or television stars. Parasocial relationships expand the social network in a way that negates the chance of rejection. For some, the one-sided nature of the relationship is a relief from strained relationships in their real life. In the past, parasocial relationships occurred predominantly with television or film celebrities, but now these relationships occur between individuals and their favourite bloggers, social media users and gamers. Reality television allows viewers to share the intimate and personal lives of television personas, and celebrities openly share their opinions and activities through various social media outlets such as Twitter and Facebook. While parasocial relationships still remain one-sided, they have transformed into more interactive environments, allowing individuals to communicate with their media personas, and increasing the intimacy and strength of the parasocial relationship.

There are similarities between parasocial relationships and more traditional social relationships. Just as relational maintenance is important in sustaining a relationship with our real-life friends and family, relational maintenance also occurs in parasocial relationships through events such as weekly viewings, blogs and the use of social media sites, such as Twitter and Facebook. Parasocial relationships are popular within these online communities. This may be due to the increased sense of 'knowing' the personas, or the perception of parasocial interactions as having a high reward and no chance of rejection.

Evaluation

- Parasocial relationships may help fight loneliness as the parasocial relationship expands individuals' social networks.
- Parasocial relationships can help teach important lessons because people are more likely to listen to the 'role model' in a parasocial relationship.
- Parasocial relationships are advantageous because of the support that the person gains from the relationship and the individual may perceive the persona as helping to shape their own identity.
- Although some parasocial relationships are pathological and a symptom of loneliness and social anxiety some psychologists believe that parasocial relationships can broaden one's social network.

Levels of parasocial relationships

Giles and Maltby said parasocial relationships can occur and progress in three levels:

- **Entertainment-social.** Fans are attracted to celebrities because it provides entertainment.
- **Intense-personal.** Fans feel a connection with the celebrity, for example feeling like they are 'soul-mates' with the celebrity.
- **Borderline pathological.** Fans in this category have uncontrollable behaviours and fantasies about their celebrity which can become borderline pathological, leading to behaviours such as stalking and obsession.

The absorption-addiction model

McCutcheon et al. (2002) suggest this model, which applies to individuals with a weak sense of identity and consists of two stages:

- **Stage 1: absorption.** The person's attention is entirely focused on the celebrity and they find out everything they can about him or her.
- **Stage 2: addiction.** The individual craves greater and greater closeness to the chosen celebrity and becomes increasingly delusional in thinking and behaviour.

This model suggests that people seek parasocial relationships to fill the dissatisfaction they feel in their own lives. This theory argues that a personal life crisis may lead an individual to move from the absorption to the addiction stage and predicts a correlation between poor psychological health and the strength of parasocial relationships.

In support of this theory, Maltby, McCutcheon, Ashe and Houran (2001) found that intense personal celebrity worship was associated with depression and anxiety. Also, Maltby et al. (2004) concluded that intense personal celebrity worship was associated with poorer mental health, and particularly with depression, anxiety, social dysfunction, stress and low life satisfaction.

Attachment theory

Keinlen (1998) and McCann (2001) suggest that fans have a tendency to create parasocial relationships with celebrities and that this is most likely to happen with people who are 'insecurely attached' because parasocial relationships do not come with the threat of disappointment and breakup.

Exam tip

Make sure you can explain the difference between the absorption stage and the addiction stage in a parasocial relationship.

The attachment theory of parasocial relationships is a psychodynamic explanation as it argues that the tendency to form parasocial relationships originates in the early childhood relationships between the child and the primary caregiver. This theory argues that those with insecure attachments are more likely to become strongly attached to celebrities and those with anxious-ambivalent attachment style are likely to be needy and clingy in their real face-to-face relationships, which makes parasocial relationships attractive to them.

Leets (1999) studied whether attachment styles influenced the extent to which individuals engage in parasocial interaction. A sample of 115 students completed the parasocial scale and two attachment-style questionnaires. Results provided evidence that attachment styles are related to parasocial behaviour. Those with anxious-ambivalent attachment styles were the most likely to form parasocial relationships, those with secure attachment styles were in the middle and insecure-avoidants were least likely to develop such relationships.

Relationships: glossary of terms

absorption-addiction model: this model of parasocial relationships suggests that people with a weak sense of self-identity seek parasocial relationships to fill the dissatisfaction they feel in their own lives. The model proposes two stages: **absorption** in which the person's attention is entirely focused on the persona and they find out everything they can about the persona, and **addiction** in which the individual craves greater closeness to the chosen persona and becomes increasingly delusional in thinking and behaviour.

attachment theory of parasocial relationships: a psychodynamic explanation proposing that the need for parasocial relationships originates in early childhood relationships between a child and the primary caregiver and that those with insecure attachments are more likely to develop parasocial relationships because these relationships do not come with the threat of disappointment and breakup.

dyadic phase: the second stage in relationship breakdown in which the dissatisfied person tells the other partner and both partners are aware that the relationship may end.

equity theory: this theory of relationship maintenance assumes that people try to ensure that their relationships are fair and that people may leave the relationship if they perceive unfairness.

evolutionary explanation: psychologists propose that mate choice is unconsciously guided by cues that indicate some survival advantage for offspring, and that because parental investment in reproduction is different for males and females, the choice and selection of a partner is different for males and females.

filter theory: the theory that three filters are important before, and at different times in, a relationship. The three filters are: social and demographic variables; similarity of attitudes and values; and complementarity of emotional needs.

gating features: the physical or material barriers that arise between people when they interact in person such as physical appearance, age, clothing, race and class distinctions.

grave dressing phase: the fourth and final stage in relationship breakdown in which both partners try to justify leaving the relationship and construct a representation of the failed relationship that presents them in favourable terms.

halo effect: if a person is physically attractive we attribute other positive characteristics to them as well.

intrapsychic phase: the first stage in relationship breakdown in which one partner may be inwardly re-evaluating the relationship in terms of the costs and benefits.

investment model: the investment model proposes three processes that are positively associated with commitment to a relationship. These are satisfaction level, the quality of alternatives and how much an individual has already invested in a relationship.

levels of parasocial relationships: entertainment-social, where people are attracted to a persona because it provides entertainment; **intense-personal**, where the individual feels a connection with the persona; **borderline pathological**, where individuals have uncontrollable and unrealistic fantasies about their persona.

matching hypothesis: the suggestion that we are attracted to people whom we perceive to be similarly attractive to ourselves because we want to avoid being rejected by potential partners who are more attractive than ourselves.

parasocial relationships: one-sided relationships, where one person extends emotional energy, interest and time, and the other party, the persona, is completely unaware of the other's existence.

parental investment: an evolutionary theory suggesting that because a female has relatively few offspring she will require a mate who is able to provide resources and thus women are attracted to males who have social and economic advantages, but that because male reproductive capacity is only limited by the number of females who are willing to reproduce with them, males will be attracted to females who show physical characteristics of good reproductive potential.

physical attractiveness: may be an important factor in interpersonal attraction because if a person is physically attractive we attribute other positive characteristics to them as well.

relationship breakdown: Duck (1999) proposed three factors to explain why relationships break down: lack of social skills; lack of stimulation leading to disinterest and eventual relationship breakdown; maintenance difficulties, e.g. if daily contact is decreased the relationship may not survive.

self-disclosure: the act of revealing ourselves, consciously or otherwise, to another person. There are two dimensions to self-disclosure — breadth and depth.

social exchange theory: the theory that relationships are based on 'exchanges' in which each person seeks to maximise their rewards and minimise their costs and thus make a profit.

social phase: the third stage in relationship breakdown in which partners inform friends and family about the problems in the relationship and others may try to help or may take sides.

virtual relationships: electronically mediated relationships in which physical attraction and eye contact are absent and in which when partners are more or less anonymous they may behave in a deindividuated and uninhibited manner.

Knowledge summary

You should be able to demonstrate knowledge and understanding of:

- evolutionary explanations for partner preferences, including the relationship between sexual selection and human reproductive behaviour
- factors affecting attraction in romantic relationships, including self-disclosure and physical attractiveness, including the matching hypothesis and filter theory
- theories of romantic relationships, including social exchange theory, equity theory and Rusbult's investment model of commitment, as well as Duck's phase model of relationship breakdown

- virtual relationships in social media, including self-disclosure in virtual relationships and the effects of absence of gating on the nature of virtual relationships
- parasocial relationships, including levels of parasocial relationships, the absorption-addiction model and the attachment theory explanation

When answering questions on relationships you will be expected to be able to illustrate your answers with knowledge and understanding from topics studied across the specification.

Stress

Stress is a type of alarm reaction, involving heightened mental and bodily states. It is both a physiological and psychological response to the environment. Thus, stress can be defined as the response that happens when we think we cannot cope with a stressor in the environment. If we think we cannot cope, we feel stress, and when we feel stress, we experience physiological changes.

The physiology of stress

Physiological explanations of stress focus on how and why the brain and nervous system respond to stressors. You need to know how the body responds to stressors, for example the role of the **autonomic nervous system** (ANS) and the **pituitary-adrenal system**. You also need to be able to describe and evaluate research into the relationship between stress and illness and the effect of stress on the **immune system**.

The general adaptation syndrome (GAS)

Selye (1956) proposed that stress leads to a depletion of the body's resources, leaving the animal vulnerable to illness. He used the word 'stress' to describe the fact that many different stimuli (e.g. fear, pain, injury) all produce the same response. He called these 'stressors' and proposed that the body reacts in the same general way to all these stressors by producing a response which helps the animal adapt to them and continue to function. Selye called this the 'general adaptation syndrome' (GAS) and identified three stages in the model:

- **Stage 1: alarm**. When we perceive a stressor, the ANS responds. Adrenaline, noradrenaline and corticosteroids (hormones) are released into the bloodstream. The bodily reaction is increased arousal levels in readiness for a physical response (fight or flight), i.e. the heart rate increases, blood pressure rises and muscles tense.
- **Stage 2: resistance**. If the stressor continues, the bodily reaction (the fight or flight response) ceases and we appear to be coping. But output from the adrenal cortex continues and the adrenal glands may become enlarged.
- **Stage 3: exhaustion**. If the stressor continues for a long time, the body is unable to cope. The body's resources are reduced but alarm signs, such as increased blood pressure, may return. The person may become depressed and unable to concentrate. The immune system may be damaged and stress-related diseases, such as stomach ulcers, high blood pressure and depression, are more likely to occur.

The hypothalamic-pituitary-adrenal system (HPA)

The HPA is activated by chronic stress (e.g. worry about the illness of a family member or even about exams). The stress response originates in the hypothalamus and includes the pituitary and adrenal glands. This HPA axis is responsible for arousing the ANS in response to a stressor.

Under stress, the sympathetic branch of the nervous system stimulates the adrenal gland to release adrenaline, noradrenaline and corticosteroids into the bloodstream. This produces the physiological reactions, such as increased heart rate and blood pressure and a dry mouth, known as the **'fight or flight' response**.

Sympathomedullary pathway (SAM)

The SAM is activated by an acute stressor (e.g. falling down).

In acute stress the the hypothalamus activates the adrenal medulla. The adrenal medulla is part of the ANS that acts as a control system generally without our conscious control. The adrenal medulla secretes the hormone adrenaline and adrenaline prepares the body for a fight or flight response. The physiological reaction includes increased heart rate, the arousal of the sympathetic nervous system and reduced activity in the parasympathetic nervous system, and changes in the body such as decreases in digestion and increases in sweating, pulse rate and blood pressure.

Once the stressor is removed (the threat is over) the parasympathetic branch of the nervous system takes control and brings the body back into a balanced state. (Figure 1 on page 34 shows a diagram of the HPA and SAM.)

Exam tip

In the exam you could be given a hypothetical situation and asked to identify whether GAS stage 1, stage 2 or stage 3 changes might occur.

Knowledge check 19

When we are in a stressful situation what causes the fight or flight response symptoms such as increased heart rate and blood pressure and a dry mouth?

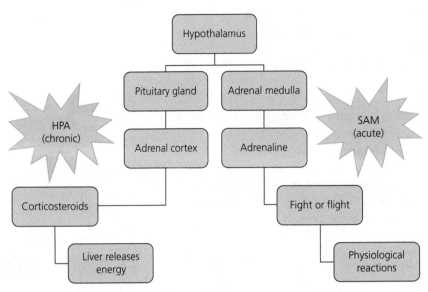

Figure 1 The hypothalamic-pituitary-adrenal system (HPA) and the sympathomedullary pathway (SAM)

The stress hormone cortisol

The stress hormone cortisol can cause damage to health because raised cortisol levels lower immune function and bone density and also increase the risk of depression and mental illness. High cortisol levels have been found to be a potential trigger for mental illness, especially in adolescence. Cortisol is released in response to fear or stress by the adrenal glands as part of the fight or flight mechanism as defined in the general adaptation syndrome (Selye 1956). Selye defined two types of stress: eustress (good stress) and distress (bad stress). Both eustress and distress release cortisol as part of the general adaption syndrome. During **distress** when cortisol is released your body becomes mobilised and ready for 'fight or flight', and unless there is some physical action (e.g. you run away from the snarling dog), cortisol levels build up in the blood which presents risk to health. In comparison, during **eustress** there is a heightened state of arousal and cortisol levels return to normal upon completion of the task.

The role of stress in illness

Stress and the immune system

The immune system comprises billions of cells that travel through the bloodstream. They are produced in the bone marrow, spleen, lymph nodes and thymus. The major type of immune cell is the white blood cell, which defends the body against antigens — bacteria, viruses and cancerous cells. Some types of immune cells produce antibodies that destroy antigens. When we are stressed, the ability of the immune system to protect us against antigens is reduced, leading to an increased likelihood of physical illness. This weakening of the immune system is called the **immunosuppressive effect of stress**. In long-term stress, such as stage 3 of Selye's GAS, increased levels of corticosteroids reduce the production of antibodies (a direct effect).

Knowledge check 20

Outline the effect of cortisol.

Research evidence

Stress and the immune system: Kiecolt-Glaser et al. (1984)

Based on the assumption that the body's response to stress reduces the effectiveness of the immune system (immunosuppression), Kiecolt-Glaser et al. aimed to establish a link between stress and reduced immune system functioning.

Aims: To look for evidence of a difference in immune response in high- and low-stress conditions, and to see whether factors such as anxiety were associated with immune system functioning.

Procedures: 75 first-year medical students (49 male and 26 female) volunteered to give blood samples 1 month before their final exams, and again after they had sat two papers on the first day of the exams. The blood samples were analysed for how much 'natural killer cell' activity was present (natural killer cells help to protect against viruses). The students also completed questionnaires to find out what other stressful events they might be experiencing.

Findings: In comparison with the first blood sample, natural killer cell activity was significantly reduced in the second sample. It was most reduced in those students who were experiencing other stressful events, and in those who reported feeling anxious and depressed.

Conclusion: Stress has an immunosuppressant effect and can be associated with reduced immune system function.

Evaluation

- The study has high external realism as the exams were real-life experiences that would have happened anyway.
- The first blood sample acted as a baseline control and the participants were being compared against themselves — this controlled for the effects of personality variables.
- It is not possible to exclude other factors that could have caused the change in the students' immune systems as other variables could not be controlled (e.g. it might have been lack of sleep due to long hours revising that affected the immune system).
- It is not possible to say how long-lasting the reduced effectiveness of the immune system might be.

Research evidence

The effect of stress on wound healing: Kiecolt-Glaser et al. (1995)

The immune system is involved in helping the body repair itself after injury. Following tissue damage (cuts and wounds), the immune system produces interleukin B that promotes healing by helping to create scar tissue.

→

Exam tip

Make sure you can explain what the immune system does and how stress affects the immune system.

Aim: To show that stress has an indirect effect on wound healing due to reduced effectiveness of the immune system.

Procedures: The study involved 13 women who cared for relatives suffering from Alzheimer's disease (the high-stress group), and a control group of 13 women who had no stressful responsibilities (the no-stress group). All the women gave skin samples, which caused skin wounds.

Findings: The wounds of the carers in the high-stress group took, on average, 9 days longer than those of the no-stress group to heal.

Conclusions: long-term stress reduces the effectiveness of the immune system to heal wounds.

Evaluation

- The study is useful to medical staff as it may explain why the wounds of some patients take longer to heal than expected.
- The sample was small and all female, and it may not be safe to generalise the findings to other populations.
- There was no baseline measure of how rapidly the wounds might have healed in the high-stress group before the onset of the stressor.

Stress and cardiovascular disorders

Cardiovascular disorders are disorders of the heart and blood vessels and are sometimes linked with stress. People who experience stress may engage in unhealthy activities, such as smoking and drinking alcohol, in an attempt to relieve the stress. These behaviours increase the likelihood that the person may develop a cardiovascular disorder, so stress may cause illness indirectly.

Long-term stress may also have a direct effect on the cardiovascular system. Stress causes high heart rate and high blood pressure. Long-term stress can damage blood vessels because adrenaline and noradrenaline contribute to increases in blood cholesterol levels, leading to blood clots and thickened arteries. Weakened or damaged blood vessels may cause haemorrhages, which in turn may lead to blockages in blood vessels, causing strokes or heart attacks.

Research evidence

The effect of stress on blood flow: Krantz et al. (1991)

This study investigated the direct effect of stress on blood flow and blood pressure. Thirty-nine participants performed a stress-inducing task (e.g. a maths test) while their blood pressure and rate of blood flow to the heart were measured. The stressful task caused a reduced blood flow to the heart and led to raised blood pressure. From this it was concluded that stress does have a direct effect on the cardiovascular system, making cardiovascular disorders more likely.

Exam tip

You should be able to explain why Kiecolt-Glaser concluded that stress has an **indirect** effect on wound healing. In this study, what did the stress have a **direct** effect on?

Knowledge check 21

Outline how stress affects the immune system.

Sources of stress

Knowledge check 22

Explain how long-term stress may cause physical illness.

Two major sources of stress are life events, and stress in the workplace.

- **Life events.** Throughout our lives we experience many changes, such as leaving home, marriage, changing employment, the birth of children and moving house. These events cause us to change the way we live, and adjusting to change may cause stress. Stress can also be caused by regular everyday hassles such as struggling to find a place to park, or being stuck in a traffic jam.
- **The workplace.** Work can be stressful. For some people, the kind of work they do, where they work and with whom they work can be a source of stress. Some of the more stressful occupations are nursing, teaching and the emergency services. Someone who is stressed at work may become ill and need to take time off.

Life changes and stress

Throughout our lives we experience changes and adjusting to change may cause stress. Psychologists have investigated how many life changes a person can experience before they run the risk of developing stress-related illness.

Research evidence

Life changes and the Social Readjustment Rating Scale (SRRS): Holmes and Rahe (1967)

Aims:

(1) To construct an instrument for measuring stress (stress was defined as the amount of life change people had experienced during a fixed period).

(2) To show that the amount of life change (i.e. the amount of stress) is related to psychological and physiological illness.

Procedures: The medical records of 5,000 patients were examined and a list was compiled of 43 kinds of life event that had taken place in the 12 months before their illnesses. One hundred people (the 'judges') were told that the life event of marriage had been rated at 500 points. They were then asked to rate how much readjustment each of the 43 life events would require 'relative to marriage'.

Findings:

(1) Death of a spouse was thought to require twice as much adjustment as marriage and was rated at 1,000 points by the judges. The average for each of the 43 life events was calculated. Holmes and Rahe could now rank the 43 life events from death of a spouse (at 1,000 points) to minor violations of the law (11 points), resulting in their Social Readjustment Rating Scale. A questionnaire was designed in which participants ticked the life events they had experienced in the last 12 months, thus giving a measure of the amount of life change (stress) they had experienced.

(2) People with high scores on the SRRS (over the previous 12 months) were likely to experience some physical illness. A person having 300 points over 12 months had an 80% chance of becoming ill — illnesses ranged from heart attacks to diabetes and sports injuries.

→

Conclusions:

(1) Stress can be objectively measured by the SRRS as a life change score.

(2) High scores on the SRRS (high-stress scores) predict physical illness, and stressful life changes cause physical illness.

Exam tip

Make sure you know what is measured by the SRRS.

Knowledge check 23

How does the SRRS measure the amount of social readjustment (life changes) an individual has experienced?

Evaluation

- The research provides an objective measure of the relationship between stress and illness. Supporting evidence was found from a study in which 2,500 navy personnel completed the SRRS before they left for a 6-month trip on board their ships. Health records were kept which found that high scores on the SRRS were correlated with physical illness.
- The experience of a life event is different for each person, e.g. some people may be distressed by divorce whereas others are relieved. Life events other than the 43 on the SRRS may also cause stress, e.g. having your home flooded.
- Most of the 43 life events are infrequent and the daily small hassles of life may be a more significant cause of stress.
- The 43 life events listed on the SRRS are only likely to be experienced by mature adults with families.

Daily hassles and stress

Some psychologists suggest that it is the daily hassles of everyday life, rather than big life changes, that are a source of stress.

DeLongis et al. (1982) theorised that it was everyday hassles that caused stress. They created a hassles scale to assess the effect of the routine problems of life, such as getting stuck in a traffic jam. The hassles scale measures positive events (uplifts) as well as hassles. In people over 45, they found that the hassles scale was a better predictor of ill health than life changes (SRRS). The frequency and intensity of hassles significantly correlated to ill health.

Research evidence

Kanner et al. (1981)

Aim: Is it daily hassles, rather than major life events, that are the most stressful? A 117 item hassles scale and a 135 uplifts scale was developed to examine the relationship between hassles and health.

Method: An opportunity sample of 100 US participants, including 52 women and 48 men, all white, well educated and middle class were asked to circle the events on both scales that they had experienced the previous month and rate each according to severity (for the hassles) and frequency (for the uplifts). A longitudinal study with repeated measures design was used and participants filled out both the life events scale and the hassles and uplifts scale. They then had their psychological symptoms of stress assessed using the Hopkins symptom checklist and the Bradburn morale scale. (Nine subjects dropped out.)

Findings: It was found that the hassles scale was a better predictor of psychological and physiological symptoms than were the life events scores. Hassles also seemed to be consistent month on month. Hassles and symptoms of stress were significantly correlated. The more hassles the participant reported the more symptoms they reported. Uplifts were positively related to reduced symptoms for women but not for men.

Conclusion: The assessment of daily hassles and uplifts may be a better approach to the prediction of stress and ill health than the life events approach.

	Daily hassles		Daily uplifts
1	Concerns about weight	1	Relating well to spouse or partner
2	Health of a family member	2	Relating well to friends
3	Rising price of common goods	3	Completing a task
4	Home maintenance	4	Feeling healthy
5	Too many things to do	5	Getting enough sleep
6	Misplacing or losing things	6	Eating out
7	Outside home maintenance	7	Meeting your responsibilities
8	Property, investment or taxes	8	Visiting, phoning or writing to someone
9	Crime	9	Spending time with the family
10	Physical appearance	10	Finding your home a pleasant environment

Daily hassles and uplifts

Exam tip

Make sure you know the difference between a life changing event and a daily hassle and can give an example of each.

Knowledge check 24

What is the difference between a life changing event and a daily hassle?

Workplace stress

Stress in the workplace can originate in six areas:

(1) Interpersonal factors. Relationships with bosses, colleagues and customers may be stressful. Good relationships with co-workers can reduce stress in the workplace; poor relationships at work can exacerbate stress.

(2) Workload and pressure. Having too much work to do and working to strict deadlines can cause stress.

(3) The physical environment. This may be noisy, hot and overcrowded, or may involve health risks and unsociable hours, such as working night shifts. Czeisler et al. (1982) researched the causes of health problems and sleep difficulties experienced by employees of a chemical plant in Utah, USA. The employees worked shifts. Czeisler recommended that the pattern of shifts should be changed to a 21-day shift rotation and always 'shift forward' (phase advance). After 9 months, job satisfaction and productivity increased.

(4) Role stress. Worry about job security or responsibility may cause stress.

(5) Role conflict. Having to express one emotion while feeling another may cause stress, e.g. in doctors, nurses, police.

(6) Control. How much control people have over how they do a job may be a factor in how stressful the job is perceived to be.

Exam tip

In the exam you could be given a description of a hypothetical workplace and be asked to identify possible causes of stress in this workplace.

Research evidence

Control and interpersonal relationships at work: Johnson and Hall (1988)

Aim: To investigate the relationship between variables in the workplace (social support, perceived control and how demanding jobs are) and the incidence of cardiovascular disease.

Procedures: Data from 14,000 male and female Swedish workers were analysed to explore the relationship between cardiovascular disease and job stress, specifically stress associated with control, demand and social support. The data included four scales of measurement:

(1) Work control, based on questions about the level of influence over the planning of work

(2) Work-related social support, based on questions about how and when workers could interact with co-workers

(3) Psychological demands of work, based on questions about how demanding the work was

(4) An indicator of cardiovascular health

Findings:

- Jobs that were perceived to be demanding but that involved low levels of control were related to increased incidences of heart disease.
- Where workers had fewer social interaction opportunities (low social support), there was an increase in cardiovascular disease in the high-demand, high-control combination.
- Low social support combined with low control increased cardiovascular disease.

Conclusion: Both social support and control are important factors in work-related stress.

Knowledge check 25

How are workload and lack of control causes of stress-related ill health?

Evaluation

- This research is useful because it shows how factors such as control and social support at work are important in understanding workplace stress.
- Self-reports may result in inaccurate descriptions of job characteristics and may be biased by personality characteristics.
- Workplaces are complex. Using objective measures of workplace stress may result in a reductionist approach that overemphasises the social context of stress.
- Qualitative research is required in order to understand the meaning of events for individuals.

Factors that may cause stress in the workplace

Role conflict in the workplace (Margolis and Kroes 1974)

This research found that when the demands of the organisation conflict with the needs of the workers, stress may result. They found that when the job requires workers to express one emotion, e.g. being calm and cheerful, while really feeling another emotion, e.g. being unhappy or worried, this causes role conflict. Nurses, teachers and paramedics are likely to suffer stress caused by role conflict.

Is having control at work important? (Marmot et al. 1997)

This research investigated whether perceived control is an important factor in work-related stress. In their study, 7,000 civil service employees who worked in London participated in a survey. Data were gathered on how senior they were (their employment grade) and how much control and support they perceived they had at work. Five years later, the medical histories of the employees were reviewed. The participants who were less senior (lower grades) and who felt they had less control and less social support were more likely to have cardiovascular disorders. It was concluded that how much control people have at work, and how much social support people receive from colleagues, may be factors in whether they suffer from stress-related illness.

Exam tip

In the exam you could be asked to apply your knowledge to suggest how to reduce stress in the workplace.

Measuring stress

Using self-report scales to measure stress

Holmes and Rahe (1967): Social Readjustment Rating Scale (SRRS) (see page 37)

The aim was to construct an instrument for measuring stress (stress was defined as the amount of life changes people had experienced during a fixed period). A questionnaire was designed in which participants ticked the life events they had experienced in the last 12 months, thus giving a measure of the amount of life change (stress). Using the SRRS, stress can be objectively measured as a life changes score. High scores on the SRRS (high-stress scores) predict physical illness, and stressful life changes cause physical illness.

Kanner et al. (1981): daily hassles and uplifts scale (see page 38)

A 117 item hassles scale and a 135 uplifts scale were developed to examine the relationship between hassles and health. A longitudinal study with repeated measures design was used and participants filled out both the life events scale and the hassles and uplifts scale. The hassles scale was a better predictor of psychological and physiological symptoms than were the life events scores and hassles and symptoms of stress were significantly correlated. The more hassles the participant reported the more symptoms they reported.

Evaluation

- Self-report scales may only be appropriate for use with specific samples of the population (e.g. the SRRS is only appropriate for use with mature adults).
- Self-report scales may lack validity — as people's feelings of stress will vary from day to day and people may over or under estimate the degree to which they are experiencing stress.

Knowledge check 26

Can you identify a sample of the population for which the SRRS may not be an appropriate way to measure stress and explain why?

Using physiological measures of stress

Skin conductance response

Skin conductance response, also known as galvanic skin response, is a method of measuring the electrical conductance of the skin, which varies depending on the amount of sweat-induced moisture on the skin. Sweat is controlled by the sympathetic nervous system, so skin conductance is used as an indication of psychological or physiological arousal. If the sympathetic branch of the autonomic nervous system is highly aroused, then sweat gland activity also increases, which in turn increases skin conductance. In this way, skin conductance can be used as a measure of emotional and sympathetic responses.

Research evidence

The effect of control in reducing stress reactions: Geer and Maisel (1972)

Aim: To see if perceived control or actual control can reduce stress reactions to adverse stimuli.

Method/procedure: Laboratory experiment in which 60 student participants were shown photographs of dead car crash victims and their stress levels were measured by galvanic skin response (GSR) and heart rate through ECG monitoring. The study employed an independent measures design with participants randomly assigned to three conditions:

- **Group 1**: were given control over how long they looked at the images for. They could press a button to terminate the image and were told a tone would precede each new image.
- **Group 2**: were warned the photos would be 60 seconds apart, they would see the picture for 35 seconds and a 10-second warning tone would precede each photo. The group had no control but did know what was happening.
- **Group 3**: were told that from time to time they would see photos and hear tones but were not given timings or any control.

Each participant was seated in a sound-proofed room and wired up to the GSR and ECG machines. The machine was calibrated for 5 minutes while the participant relaxed and a baseline measurement was then taken. Instructions were read over an intercom. Each photo was preceded with a 10-second tone and then flashed up and the photograph disappeared either when the button was pressed (Group 1) or after the predetermined length of time (Groups 2 and 3). The GSR was taken at the onset of the tone, during the second half of the tone and in response to the photo.

Results: ECG recordings were discarded as they appeared inaccurate. Group 1 (who could control how long they saw the image for) experienced the least stress. The predictability group (Group 2) showed higher stress, as they knew what was coming, but did not have any control over the photograph. Group 3 (no control) showed the highest stress levels.

Conclusion: Having control over your environment can reduce stress responses.

Stress hormones in urine: Johansson et al. (1978)

Aim: To investigate whether work stressors such as repetitiveness, machine-regulated pace of work and high levels of responsibility increase stress-related physiological arousal and stress-related illness.

Procedures: The researchers identified a high-risk group of 14 'finishers' in a Swedish sawmill. Their job was to finish off the wood at the last stage of processing timber. The work was machine-paced, isolated, very repetitive yet highly skilled, and the finishers' productivity determined the wage rates for the entire factory. The 14 finishers were compared with a low-risk group of 10 cleaners, whose work was more varied, largely self-paced and allowed more socialising with other workers. Levels of stress-related hormones (adrenaline and noradrenaline) in the urine were measured on work days and rest days. Records were kept of stress-related illness and absenteeism.

Findings: The high-risk group of 14 finishers secreted more stress hormones (adrenaline and noradrenaline) on work days than on rest days, and higher levels than the control group. The high-risk group of finishers also showed significantly higher levels of stress-related illness, such as headaches, and higher levels of absenteeism than the low-risk group of cleaners.

Conclusions: A combination of work stressors, especially repetitiveness, machine-pacing of work and high levels of responsibility, lead to chronic (long-term) physiological arousal which leads to stress-related illness and absenteeism.

Lorry drivers' work stress evaluated by catecholamines excreted in urine: Beek et al. (1995)

Aims: To evaluate lorry drivers' work stress by measurement of adrenaline and noradrenaline excreted in the urine, and to find out which factors in their working situation are related to the excretion rates of these catecholamines.

Procedures: The urinary excretion of adrenaline and noradrenaline of 32 lorry drivers, who also had loading and unloading activities to perform, was studied for one working day and one rest day. Each driver was asked to provide six urine samples on both days.

Findings: For all samples, except the first (overnight) sample, the excretion rates of both catecholamines on the working day were higher than those on the rest day.

Conclusion: The excretion rates of adrenaline and, especially, noradrenaline on the working day were higher than those found in earlier studies among professional drivers and insufficient recovery took place after the work was ended.

> ### Evaluation
>
> - Physiological measurements give scientific and objective data that can be used to make comparisons such as before and after stress treatment.
> - Physiological measurements of stress are reductionist — as they reduce the psychological and subjective experience of stress to simplistic single factor biological measurements.

Exam tip

Make sure you can evaluate the strengths and limitations of using self-report scales and/or physiological methods to measure stress.

Individual differences in stress

There are individual differences in the extent to which people experience stress and no two people respond to stressors in the same way. Some people seem to thrive on lifestyles that others would find stressful. Psychologists research how personality factors may be involved in how people respond to stressors.

Type A and B personalities

Cardiologists Friedman and Rosenman (1974) defined two types of behaviour pattern, Type A and Type B, and studied their relation to coronary heart disease (CHD).

Type A behaviour: Type A people move, walk, eat and talk rapidly, and try to do two or more things at one time. In personality, Type A people are competitive and tend to judge themselves by the number of successes they have rather than the quality of their successes. Type A individuals are hard-driving, impatient and aggressive. They tend to be achievement-oriented and hostile. In physiology, Type A people have a higher level of cholesterol and fat in their bloodstream, a more difficult time getting the cholesterol out of their bloodstream and a greater likelihood of clotting within the arteries.

Type B behaviour: Type B people seldom feel any sense of time urgency or impatience, are not preoccupied with their achievements or accomplishments and seldom become angry or irritable. They tend to enjoy their recreation, are free of guilt about relaxing, and they work calmly and smoothly.

Exam tip

In the exam you could be given a description of a fictitious person and be asked to identify whether they are a Type A or Type B personality. Make sure you can list the personality characteristics of both Type A and Type B.

Research evidence

Type A personality: Friedman and Rosenman (1974)

Aim: Based on their observations of patients who displayed the common Type A behaviour pattern of impatience, competitiveness and hostility, Friedman and Rosenman aimed to test their belief that Type A personalities were more prone to CHD than Type B personalities.

Procedures: The sample comprised 3,000 male volunteers, all from California, USA, aged between 39 and 59, who were healthy at the start of the study. Personality type was established through the use of a structured interview and observations of the participants' behaviour during the interview. The interviewer interrupted the interview from time to time so that the Type A individuals would become annoyed. The answers to questions and behavioural responses were used to assess participants' impatience, competitiveness and hostility.

Findings: $8^1/_2$ years later, 257 of the men in the sample were diagnosed as having CHD — 70% of those with CHD had been classified as Type A.

The Type A men were also found to have higher levels of adrenaline and cholesterol. Twice as many Type A men had died as compared with Type Bs. Type As also had higher blood pressure, higher cholesterol and other symptoms of CHD. Type As were more likely to smoke and have a family history of CHD, both of which would increase their own risk.

Conclusion: Type A personality is associated with illness and symptoms of CHD. Because Type A is also linked to other factors that cause CHD, such as smoking, it is not certain whether Type A is a direct or indirect cause of CHD.

Evaluation

- The study has high external validity because it was a long-term study with a large sample having a baseline measure (all the men were free of CHD at the start of the study).
- The study is useful because it showed how psychological factors such as personality can be related to physiological factors such as CHD.
- The sample was both ethnocentric and gender-biased (all males from the USA) and as such cannot be generalised to females.
- The findings of Williams (2000) support Friedman and Rosenman in their description of Type A personalities as hostile. In Williams' study, 13,000 participants completed questionnaires asking about their feelings of anger, and the participants' responses were rated for anger scores. Six years later, those with high anger scores were significantly more likely to have suffered a heart attack.

Type C personality

This personality type comprises people who think systematically and analytically and who tend to be problem solvers because they focus on details. Highly sensitive, they are also known for other character traits like the avoidance of human interaction. The Type C personality has difficulty expressing emotion, particularly negative emotions such as anger. Individuals with Type C personality traits may display pathological niceness and conflict avoidance and compliance. According to Temoshock (1987), because of the tendency to suppress or inhibit their emotions Type C personalities are 'cancer prone' because they respond to stress with a sense of helplessness. In support of this, Morris et al. (1981) found a link between people who tended to suppress their anger and the increased incidence of cancer.

Research evidence

Helgeson and Fritz (1999) studied nearly 300 patients receiving treatment for blocked arteries. Six months later, they found that those patients who were lowest in 'cognitive adaptation' were three times more likely to have experienced a new coronary event. High cognitive adaptation included an ability to develop a **positive outlook about one's medical condition and a sense of control** in most situations. They concluded that the 'pessimist personality' is more likely to become ill as a result of stress.

Exam tip

Make sure you can describe how Friedman and Rosenman measured the link between Type A personality and stress-related illness.

Knowledge check 27

Why is a Type B personality less likely to suffer stress-related illness?

Knowledge check 28

Briefly describe the personality characteristics of the Type A personality.

The hardy personality

Kobasa (1979) proposed that some people are better able to deal with stress (the hardy personality) and that all people could learn to behave in this way in order to cope better. The key traits of a hardy personality, known as the three Cs, are having:

- a strong sense of personal *control*
- a strong sense of purpose (*commitment*)
- the ability to see problems positively, as *challenges* to be overcome rather than as stressors

According to Kobasa, hardy personalities see themselves as the managers of their environment. They are committed to face problems and will not stop until they find resolutions to these. In addition, hardy people view change not as a threat, but as a challenge to be met and overcome — maintained rather than damaged.

Research evidence

Kobasa undertook research which aimed to test any link between a hardy personality and stress levels. The stress levels of 800 business executives were measured using Holmes and Rahe's SRRS. Hardiness was also assessed using a 'hardiness' test.

Findings: 150 of the executives had high levels of stress and those with low levels of illness (and therefore stress) were more likely to have scored high on the hardy personality test.

Conclusion: Having a hardy personality can reduce the levels of stress — if a person is classified as a hardy individual, he or she is able to respond to stress in a more positive way.

Exam tip

Make sure you can explain how the three hardy personality characteristics may influence how a person reacts to stressful situations.

Evaluation

- There are issues of validity and reliability with using psychometric tests to measure personality.
- The link between stress levels and personality types is correlational and thus cannot be said to be causational.
- Research cannot show that Type A personality causes CHD. It may be that Type A behaviours develop as a result of long-term stress.
- Categorising men (and women) into 'personality types' is reductionist and there are ethical issues concerning the suggestion that the personality traits of a person are related to the development of cancer.

Managing and coping with stress

Physiological approaches to stress management help people cope with stress by changing the way the body responds to stress — they focus on the reduction of physical symptoms of stress. Psychological approaches to helping people cope with stress focus on encouraging people to think about their problems in a different way and on encouraging people to deal with the causes of their stress.

Psychologists categorise coping strategies as physiological or psychological and/or emotion-focused or problem-focused:

- Emotion-focused strategies attempt to reduce the symptoms of anxiety by taking a physiological approach, for example anti-anxiety drugs may be used.
- Problem-focused strategies attempt to change how people respond to stressors, by using cognitive therapies or by encouraging people to increase their social support.

Drug therapy

Drugs aim to reduce the physiological, or bodily, response to stress. Two drugs which do this are benzodiazepine and beta-blockers.

Benzodiazepine is an anti-anxiety (anxiolytic) drug and its brand names include Librium and Valium. These drugs slow down the activity of the central nervous system (CNS) and reduce anxiety by enhancing the activity of a natural biochemical substance, gamma-amino-butyric-acid (GABA). GABA is the body's natural form of anxiety relief. It also reduces **serotonin** activity. Serotonin is a neurotransmitter and people with anxiety need to reduce their levels of serotonin.

Beta-blockers act on the sympathetic nervous system (SNS) rather than the brain. They reduce heart rate and blood pressure and thus reduce the harmful effects of stress.

Evaluation

Advantages of drugs
- They are quick and effective and reduce the physiological effects of stress.
- People prefer drug therapies to psychological therapies because 'taking a pill is easy'.
- They do not require people to change the way they think or behave.
- They can be used in conjunction with psychological methods.

Limitations of drugs
- All drugs have side-effects. Benzodiazepines can cause drowsiness and may affect memory.
- Long-term use of drugs can lead to physical and psychological dependency.
- They treat the symptoms of stress but most stresses are psychological and drugs do not address the causes of the problem.

Biofeedback

Biofeedback works because our minds can influence the automatic functions of our bodies. Using a special machine, people can learn to control processes such as heart rate and blood pressure. Biofeedback machines provide information about the systems in the body that are affected by stress.

The electromyogram (EMG) measures muscle tension. Electrodes are placed on your skin and when tension is detected, the machine gives you a signal. As you become aware of this internal process, you can learn techniques to control tension. Galvanic skin response (GSR) training devices measure electrical conductance in the skin. A tiny electrical current is run through your skin and the machine measures changes

Knowledge check 29

Explain the difference between physiological and psychological methods of managing stress.

Exam tip

Make sure you can name two drugs that can be used to reduce the physical symptoms of stress.

Knowledge check 30

Explain how one drug treatment reduces the physiological symptoms of stress.

Knowledge check 31

List two advantages of using drugs to treat stress.

in sweat gland ducts. The more emotionally aroused (stressed) you are, the more active your sweat glands are, and the greater the electrical conductivity of your skin.

There are four stages in learning biofeedback:

- The person is attached to a machine that monitors changes in heart rate and blood pressure and gives feedback.
- The person learns to control the symptoms of stress by deep breathing and muscle relaxation; this slows down their heart rate, making them feel more relaxed.
- The biofeedback from the machine acts like a reward and encourages the person to repeat the breathing techniques.
- Through practice, the person learns to repeat the breathing techniques in stressful situations.

Exam tip

Make sure you can suggest, and give an example of, what biological information is 'fed back' to the patient.

Evaluation

Advantages of biofeedback
- There are no side-effects.
- It reduces symptoms and gives people a sense of control.
- The learned techniques can be generalised to other stressful situations.
- It is more effective if combined with psychological therapies that encourage people to think about the causes of their stress and how their behaviour may contribute to it.

Limitations of biofeedback
- It requires specialist equipment and expert supervision.
- It requires the stressed person to commit time and effort.
- Anxious people may find learning biofeedback techniques difficult.

Knowledge check 32

Outline the processes involved when biofeedback is used to treat stress.

Stress inoculation therapy (Meichenbaum 1985)

Stress inoculation therapy (SIT) is a 'talking therapy' and a form of cognitive behavioural therapy (CBT). The aim of SIT is to prepare people to cope with stress in a similar way to an injection preventing a disease. Training people to deal with stress before it becomes a problem involves three stages:

- **Conceptualisation.** The clients identify and express their feelings and fears and are educated about stress. They are encouraged to re-live stressful situations, analysing what was stressful about them and how they attempted to deal with them.
- **Skill acquisition and rehearsal.** The clients are taught how to relax, how to think differently about stressors and how to express their emotions as well as specific skills such as communication skills, time management or study skills.
- **Application and follow-through.** The trainer guides the clients through progressively more threatening situations so that they can apply their newly acquired skills. The techniques become reinforced and this makes the practice self-sustaining.

Research evidence

A study of stress inoculation

Raymond Novaco (1975, 1977) demonstrated the usefulness of stress inoculation training and relaxation in helping people to control anger. He trained patients who self-identified and who were clinically assessed as having serious problems controlling anger. The subjects learned about the role of arousal and cognitive processes in feelings of anger and participants practised the techniques while imagining and role playing realistic anger situations arranged in a hierarchy from least to most provoking. When provoked in a laboratory they were able to control their anger as measured by both their blood pressure and their self-reports.

Exam tip

In the exam you will be expected to know the processes involved in stress inoculation therapy.

Evaluation

Advantages of stress inoculation

- Meichenbaum's model focuses on both the nature of the stress problem (enabling clients to more realistically appraise their life) and the ways of coping with stress (giving clients more understanding of the strengths and limitations of specific techniques).
- It has been effective in a variety of stressful situations, ranging from anxiety about mathematics in college students, managing hypertension in all age groups and stress management in general. It has been successfully combined with other treatment methods to alleviate stress.
- It focuses on the cause of stress and on ways of coping with it.
- It is effective for both short- and long-term stressors and can be combined with other treatment methods.
- The increased feelings of 'being in control' and improved communication and time-management skills lead to increased self-confidence and self-efficacy.
- There are no physiological side-effects.

Limitations of stress inoculation

- It may only be successful with patients who are already determined to make the time and effort to help themselves.
- The research findings are based on a narrow sample (mainly white, middle-class, well-educated people); thus they may not generalise to other populations.

Knowledge check 33

Outline how stress inoculation therapy (SIT) is used to help people manage stress.

Increasing hardiness (Kobasa 1977)

The aim of increasing hardiness is to encourage people to respond to stressors in a positive manner instead of perceiving them as disasters, and to teach the behavioural, physiological and cognitive skills that enable them to cope with stressors. Hardiness training involves three stages:

- **Focusing.** Patients are taught to recognise the signs of stress, such as muscle tension and tiredness, and to identify the sources of the stress.

- **Re-living stressful encounters.** Patients are asked to re-live stressful situations and to analyse these situations so that they can learn from past experience.
- **Self-improvement.** Patients use the insights gained to help them see stressors as challenges that can be coped with, leading to improved self-confidence and an enhanced sense of personal control.

Evaluation

Advantages of increasing hardiness

- Evidence suggests this approach is effective. Williams et al. (1992) found that 'high' hardy people use more problem-focused and support-seeking measures when dealing with stress than 'low' hardy people, who tend to use avoidance and wishful thinking. Hardiness is associated with successful coping strategies.
- As with stress inoculation, hardiness training focuses on coping with the causes of stress.
- It can be combined with other treatment methods and improves self-confidence and self-efficacy.

Limitations of increasing hardiness

- The research findings are based on an all-male sample and may not generalise to females.
- It may only be successful with patients who see stress as a challenge to be coped with.
- The concept of hardiness is complex, and in stressful situations even hardy personalities may succumb to anxiety and negative thinking.

Gender differences and stress

Gender may be an important factor in stress:

- Women are biologically more able to cope with stress.
- Women are socialised to cope better with stress.
- Women tend to drink and smoke less and may do less stressful work.

From an **evolutionary (biological) perspective**, men should respond to situations of danger with the 'fight or flight' arousal response, whereas women should respond by looking after young ones and each other. Research suggests that females are more likely to deal with stress by nurturing those around them and reaching out to others but that males are more likely to hide away or start a confrontation.

From a **social perspective**, males and females are socialised in different ways. Women learn to use social networks more and this may reduce their stress. They are taught to think about social conflict situations differently. Vögele et al. (1997) proposed that females learn to control their anger and react more calmly in stressful situations, but males learn that anger is an acceptable response and feel stress if they have to suppress anger. According to Billings and Moos (1981), when coping with stress, women tend to use more **emotion-focused strategies** than men who use **problem-focused coping strategies**.

Emotion-focused stress management

There are many ways of coping with stress. Their effectiveness depends on the type of stressor, the particular individual and the circumstances. Lazarus and Folkman (1984) suggested there are two types of coping responses — emotion-focused and problem-focused.

Emotion-focused coping involves trying to reduce the negative emotional responses associated with stress such as embarrassment, fear, anxiety, depression and frustration. This may be the only realistic option when the source of stress is outside the person's control.

Emotion-focused strategies include:

- keeping busy to take your mind off the issue
- letting off steam to other people
- ignoring the problem in the hope that it will go away
- distracting yourself

Evaluation

- Emotion-focused strategies are often less effective than using problem-focused methods. Epping-Jordan et al. (1994) found that patients with cancer who used avoidance strategies, e.g. denying they were very ill, deteriorated more quickly than those who faced up to their problems.
- Emotion-focused strategies do not provide a long-term solution, but can be effective if the source of stress is outside the person's control.

Problem-focused stress management

Problem-focused coping targets the causes of stress in practical ways. This tackles the problem that is causing the stress, consequently directly reducing the stress. Problem-focused strategies aim to remove or reduce the cause of the stressor. Strategies include:

- **taking control**, which involves changing the relationship between yourself and the source of stress, for example removing yourself from the source of stress (e.g. leaving a stressful job)
- **information seeking**, a cognitive response to stress as the individual tries to understand the situation and puts into place cognitive strategies to avoid it in future
- **evaluating the pros and cons** of different ways of dealing with the stressor

Evaluation

- Usually, problem-focused coping is best, as it removes the stressor and provides a long-term solution.
- It is not always possible to use problem-focused strategies. For example, when someone dies, problem-focused strategies may not be helpful for the bereaved because dealing with the feeling of loss requires emotion-focused coping.
- It will not work in any situation where it is beyond the individual's control to remove the source of stress.
- Not all people are able to take control of a situation and people with an external locus of control or low self-esteem typically use emotion-focused coping strategies.

Research evidence

Gender and stress

Pilar Matud, M. (2004) researched gender differences in stress and coping strategies in a sample of 2,816 people (1,566 women and 1,250 men) aged between 18 and 65 years old.

The results indicated that the women scored significantly higher than the men in chronic stress and minor daily stressors. Although there was no difference in the number of life events experienced in the previous 2 years, the women rated their life events as more negative and less controllable than the men. Gender differences were found with the women listing family and health-related events more frequently than the men, whereas men listed relationship, finance and work-related events. The women scored significantly higher than the men on emotional and avoidance coping styles and lower on rational and detachment coping. The men were found to have more emotional inhibition than the women. The results suggest that women suffer more stress than men and their coping style is more emotion-focused than that of men.

> **Exam tip**
>
> Make sure you know the difference between emotion-focused and problem-focused ways of coping with stress.

Social support

Research suggests that emotional support may play a significant role in protecting individuals from the effects of stress. Social support moderates vulnerability to stressful situations because when people have others to turn to, they are psychologically better able to handle stressors, such as unemployment, marital disruption and the everyday problems of living.

Researchers also make a distinction between perceived and received support. **Perceived support** refers to a recipient's subjective judgement that he or she will be offered effective help during times of need. **Received support** refers to specific supportive actions (e.g. advice or reassurance) offered during times of need. Support can come from many sources, such as family, friends, pets and neighbours.

There are four common types of social support:

- **Emotional support (esteem support)** is the offering of empathy, concern, affection, love, trust, acceptance, encouragement or caring. Providing emotional support can let the individual know that he or she is valued (esteem support).
- **Instrumental support** is the provision of financial assistance or services. This form of social support is the concrete and direct ways people assist others.
- **Informational support** is the provision of advice, guidance or useful information to help someone solve a problem.
- **Companionship support** is the type of support that gives someone a sense of social belonging.

> **Exam tip**
>
> You could be asked to give examples of each type of social support and explain how the four types of social support differ.

Research evidence

Social support

Social support may help people cope with stress because it provides companionship during which people can share their problems with others. Wexler-Morrison et al. (1991) studied 133 women diagnosed as suffering from breast cancer and found that those having a network of social support survived longer. The researchers suggested that social support may be effective because friends provide information and encouragement, and also because 'sharing a problem' acts as a 'buffer' to guard against and reverse the effects of stress.

Quick and Quick (1984) suggest that employers can help provide social support systems by (a) organising workers in teams or work groups, (b) providing facilities for recreation during lunchtime or other non-work hours, such as arranging social events for workers and their families at weekends, (c) providing counselling services to help stressed employees.

Taylor et al. (1986) studied the effectiveness of different types of social support given to cancer patients. They found that the effects of the helpfulness depended on who the helper was. For example: patients appreciated information and advice from physicians but not from family members; patients valued a spouse's 'being there' but not a doctor's or nurse's mere presence. Also, attempts at support can increase anxiety — for example, if you prefer to attend a medical appointment alone, your mother's insistence on accompanying you might cause you to feel anxious, not relaxed.

> **Exam tip**
>
> Make sure you can suggest why it may be difficult to gain a valid measure of social support and/or the effects of social support.

Stress: glossary of terms

benzodiazepine: an anti-anxiety drug that slows down the activity of the central nervous system (CNS) and reduces anxiety by enhancing the activity of a natural biochemical substance, gamma-amino-butyric-acid (GABA), which is the body's natural form of anxiety relief.

beta blockers: drugs that act on the sympathetic nervous system (SNS) rather than the brain to reduce heart rate and blood pressure and thus reduce the harmful effects of stress.

biofeedback: biofeedback machines provide information about the systems in the body that are affected by stress such as muscle tension. Electrodes are placed on the skin and when tension is detected, the machine gives a signal and as the person becomes aware of the biological changes they learn techniques to control tension.

biological approaches to stress management: the use of techniques, such as drugs and biofeedback, to change the activity of the body's stress-response system.

cardiovascular disorders: disorders of the heart and blood vessels; for instance, physical damage to the blood-supply system that may in turn lead to the blocking of a blood vessel or vessels.

control: the ability to anticipate events that may happen as well as perceiving that one is able to control the events. The most stressful situations seem to be those in which we feel helpless, believing that nothing we do will change the outcome of events.

cortisol: the stress hormone cortisol can cause damage to health because raised cortisol levels lower immune function. Cortisol is released in response to fear or stress by the adrenal glands as part of the fight or flight mechanism.

esteem support: the type of social support such as empathy, concern, affection, love, trust, acceptance, encouragement or caring that shows the individual that he or she is valued.

general adaptation syndrome: the theory that there are three stages in our response to long-term stress: the alarm stage, in which the sympathetic branch of the autonomic nervous system is activated; the resistance stage, in which the body attempts to cope by maintaining the same level of arousal; and the exhaustion stage, in which the body's resources and defence against the stressor become exhausted.

hardy personality: personality traits such as taking control of life events, seeing stressors or problems as challenges to be overcome, and being committed to solving problems or 'seeing things through'.

hassles and uplifts: the annoying events in daily life that cause stress and the pleasurable events that reduce stress levels.

immune system: a system of cells within the body that is concerned with fighting viruses and bacteria. White blood cells (leucocytes) identify and kill foreign bodies (antigens).

instrumental support: the type of social support that is concrete and direct and that offers financial assistance or services to others.

life changes: events (e.g. divorce, bereavement, change of job) that cause a person to make a significant adjustment to aspects of their life. These types of life change can be seen as significant sources of stress.

psychological approaches to stress management: the use of techniques such as cognitive behavioural therapies (e.g. stress inoculation) to help people cope better with stressful situations, or to change the way they perceive the demands of a stressful situation.

Social Readjustment Rating Scale (SRRS): a standardised questionnaire used to measure stress caused by life changes.

stress: a characteristic of the environment, for instance workplace stress, or a situation in which a person perceives they are unable to cope with the demands of what is happening; or the response of the body to a stressful situation.

stress inoculation therapy (SIT): a 'talking therapy' and a form of cognitive behavioural therapy (CBT). The aim of SIT is to prepare people to cope with stress in a similar way to an injection preventing a disease.

stress management: the different ways by which people try to cope with the negative effects of stress. They are defined as taking the physical approach, when we try to change the body's response to stress, or as the psychological approach, when we try to change the way we react to a stressful situation.

stressor: an event that causes a stress reaction in the body. Stressors include life events, such as divorce, and workplace stress.

Type A personality: personality type characterised by behaviour such as walking, eating and talking rapidly, and trying to do two or more things at one time, and by personality traits such as being competitive, hard-driving, impatient and aggressive. In physiology, Type A people have a higher level of cholesterol and fat in their bloodstream and a greater likelihood of clotting within the arteries.

workplace stressor: an aspect of working life, such as work overload or role ambiguity, that we experience as stressful and that causes a stress reaction in our body.

Knowledge summary

You should be able to demonstrate knowledge and understanding of:
- the physiology of stress, including general adaptation syndrome, the hypothalamic pituitary-adrenal system, the sympathomedullary pathway and the role of cortisol
- the role of stress in illness, including the effect of stress on the immune system and on cardiovascular disorders
- sources of stress, such as life changes and daily hassles, and stress in the workplace including the effects of workload and control
- measuring stress by using self-report scales (Social Readjustment Rating Scale and hassles and uplifts scale) and by using physiological measures, including skin conductance response

- individual differences in stress, especially personality types A, B and C and associated behaviours, and the hardy personality with its characteristics of commitment, challenge and control
- managing and coping with stress — treating stress with drug therapy (e.g. benzodiazepines, beta blockers), or by stress inoculation therapy and biofeedback
- gender differences in coping with stress
- the role of social support in coping with stress and the types of social support

When answering questions on stress you will be expected to be able to illustrate your answers with knowledge and understanding from topics studied across the specification.

Aggression

In psychology, the term aggression refers to a range of behaviours that can result in physical and psychological harm to oneself, others or objects in the environment. Aggression can take a variety of forms, including physical, verbal and emotional, and aggressive behaviour can serve different purposes such as to express anger or hostility, to assert dominance, to intimidate or threaten, as a response to fear and to compete with others.

Neural and hormonal mechanisms in aggression

The limbic system

The limbic system is a set of evolutionarily primitive brain structures located on top of the brainstem and under the cortex. Limbic system structures are involved in many of our emotions and motivations, particularly the 'survival' emotions of fear and anger, and emotions related to sexual behaviour. Certain structures of the limbic system are involved in aggression:

■ The **amygdala** is an almond-shaped mass of nuclei involved in emotional responses, hormonal secretions and memory. It has been shown to be an area that causes aggression. Stimulation of the amygdala results in increased aggressive behaviour, while damage to this area reduces aggression.

■ The **hypothalamus** is about the size of a pea and is believed to serve a regulatory role in aggression. It has been shown to cause aggressive behaviour when electrically stimulated and it has receptors that help determine aggression levels based on their interactions with the neurotransmitters serotonin and vasopressin.

Serotonin and aggression

Serotonin is a neurotransmitter and **low levels of serotonin** appear to be linked with aggressive behaviour. The link between serotonin and aggression is tested through comparing levels of the serotonin metabolite 5-HIAA in participants' cerebrospinal fluid to a history of aggressive behaviour or actual aggression. If serotonin plays a key in aggression, researchers would expect to see **reduced levels of 5-HIAA** in more aggressive people.

Research evidence

Stanley et al. (2000) compared the cerebrospinal fluid concentrations of 5-HIAA in aggressive and non-aggressive psychiatric patients. They found that aggressive participants had lower levels of 5-HIAA than the non-aggressive ones.

Davidson, Putnam and Larson (2000) suggest that serotonin provides an inhibitory function — in other words, moderate to high levels of serotonin would prevent high aggression levels. The researchers found that tame domestic pets have much higher levels of serotonin because they do not need to be aggressive.

Testosterone and aggression

Testosterone is a male sex hormone (androgen) which has been heavily implicated in aggressive behaviour and two models are proposed to explain how testosterone influences aggression:

■ The **basal model of testosterone** proposes that testosterone causes a change in a person's dominance and that the more testosterone someone has, the more competitive and dominant they will become.

■ The **reciprocal model of testosterone** proposes that testosterone levels are influenced by the level of dominance that an individual has.

Research evidence

Wagner et al. (1979) conducted correlational research using mice. They found that overall levels of aggression in mice that had been castrated tended to reduce, but that giving a castrated mouse testosterone led to aggression.

Mazur and Booth (1998) support the basal model of testosterone. They conducted a meta-analysis of research into testosterone and found that men with higher levels of testosterone were more likely to divorce or remain single, be arrested for major offences, buy/sell stolen property and use weapons in fights.

Mazur and Booth (1998) also found support for the reciprocal model of testosterone. In a study looking at 2,100 air force veterans over a 10-year period, in which testosterone levels were measured four times (during medical exams) in the 10 years, testosterone levels were found to vary — reducing when the men were married but increasing upon divorce.

Dabbs (1987) investigated whether male criminals who had higher levels of testosterone had committed more violent crimes. A sample of 88 inmates, aged between 18 and 23, was studied at a state prison in the USA. Inmates were rated on how tough they were by the guards and then they were split into four categories: 25 bo-hogs (tough inmates), 19 scrubs (weak inmates), 29 cell block (in-between) and 15 'cutters' (prisoners who self-harm). Findings were that the bo-hogs' testosterone level average was (at 8.7) significantly higher than the scrubs' average testosterone level (at 6.8). Of the 11 inmates with the highest testosterone levels, 10 had committed violent crimes, but of the 11 inmates with the lowest testosterone levels, 9 had committed non-violent crimes. The researchers concluded that there was a positive relationship between testosterone levels and violent crime.

Knowledge check 34

Explain what MAO-A stands for.

Exam tip

Can we be sure that when the testosterone levels were measured in the Dabbs study they were the same as the levels of testosterone when the men committed their crimes? You need to be able to explain why or why not.

Evaluation

Serotonin and/or testosterone studies only show a correlation between neural and hormonal levels and aggression so it is not possible to say that serotonin or testosterone levels cause aggressive behaviour. In Simpson (2001) testosterone is only one of many factors that influence aggression and the effects of environmental stimuli have been found to correlate more strongly.

Giving a biological cause for aggressive behaviour is reductionist and deterministic as even if low levels of serotonin or high levels of testosterone increase the risk of aggression, aggressive behaviour is usually a response to environmental factors. (This also links to the issue of nature or nurture as a cause of behaviour.)

Genetic factors in aggression

Monoamine oxidase A, also known as **MAO-A**, is an enzyme that in humans is encoded by the MAO-A gene. Mutation in the MAO-A gene results in monoamine oxidase deficiency. Monoamine oxidases (MAOs) are enzymes that are involved in the breakdown of neurotransmitters such as serotonin, dopamine and norepinephrine and can influence the feelings and behaviour of individuals.

One version of the MAO-A gene has been referred to as the **warrior gene**. There are several different variations of the gene and a connection between a version of the MAO-A gene (3R) and several types of antisocial behaviour has been found. Research has shown that people with the low activity MAO-A gene showed higher levels of aggression than individuals with the high activity MAO-A gene and that low activity MAO-A could significantly predict aggressive behaviour in a high provocation situation. Also, low MAO-A activity in combination with abuse experienced during childhood results in an increased risk of adult aggressive behaviour.

Research evidence

Mice that lacked a functional MAO-A gene exhibited increased aggression towards intruder mice. Types of aggression exhibited included territorial aggression, predatory aggression and isolation-induced aggression.

Brunner (1993) aimed to identify whether there is a link between genetic abnormality and criminal behaviour. He studied 5 males from the same family in the Netherlands who had all committed aggressive violent crimes, including impulsive aggression, arson and rape. They were all affected by borderline retardation and demonstrated abnormal and violent behaviour. Urine samples and blood samples were collected over a 24-hour period for DNA analysis. The findings were disturbed monoamine metabolism and a deficit of MAO-A. Brunner concluded that impaired metabolism of serotonin was likely to be involved in mental retardation, which could be linked to aggressive behaviour.

Brunner's research formed the basis for **Brunner syndrome**. This is a rare genetic disorder caused by a mutation in the MAO-A gene leading to MAO-A deficiency, which is associated with a behavioural phenotype that includes disturbed regulation of impulsive aggression. It is characterised by lower than average IQ (typically about 85) and problematic impulsive behaviour (e.g. arson and violence), as well as sleep disorders and mood swings. It was identified in 14 males from one family in 1993 and has since been discovered in additional families.

Mednick et al. (1987) studied the criminal records of Danish children adopted outside their biological family between 1924 and 1947. Having a criminal biological father increased the risk of criminality, but the highest risk was for those who had a criminal biological father and a criminal adoptive father.

> **Exam tip**
>
> Nature or nurture — can you explain why it is difficult to separate genetic influences on aggressive behaviour from environmental influences?

Evaluation

- **Reductionism:** giving a genetic explanation for aggressive behaviour reduces complex behaviour to simple biological facts and ignores psychological evidence that suggests aggressive behaviour can be learned.
- **Deterministic** (biological determinism): this gives a genetic explanation for aggressive behaviour suggesting that people do not have the free will to choose not to behave aggressively.
- **Nature or nurture**: genes are likely to increase the risk of aggression, but only when combined with environmental factors.
- The results of research on mice and other animals cannot be applied to explain human aggression.
- Heritability studies provide limited support for a genetic contribution to aggression because they usually study criminality rather than aggression and not all crime is violent or aggressive.

Ethological and evolutionary explanations for aggression

Ethological explanation

Ethology is the study of animals in their natural environment. Ethologists are interested in how animal behaviours increase an animal's chance of survival and the reproduction of the species. Konrad Lorenz proposed that aggression evolved in all animals (including humans) because it is adaptive, because the most aggressive animals control access to resources such as mates, food and territory. Lorenz proposed that certain environmental signals (e.g. the sight of a rival male) acts as a releaser of action specific energy.

Ethologists propose that much animal behaviour is:

■ instinctive and occurring in every member of the same species
■ species specific and stereotyped
■ not learned

For ethologists, instinct means a series of predictable behaviours in **fixed action patterns**. Such fixed action pattern behaviours are only acted when a precise signal known as an **innate releasing mechanism** (IRM) is present. An example of an IRM is the gaping-beak movement performed by newly hatched chicks, which stimulates the parent bird to regurgitate to feed the offspring. An IRM is an external 'sign', but fixed action pattern behaviour may also require internal stimulation, for example hunger or the sex drive during mating.

Fixed action patterns

Lea (1984) described six characteristics of fixed action patterns:

(1) Stereotyped — the behaviour always occurs in the same form.

(2) Universal — the behaviour is found throughout the species.

(3) Independence of experience — the behaviour is not learned.

(4) Ballistic — once it starts the behaviour cannot be stopped.

(5) Singleness of purpose — the behaviour is used in one context only.

(6) Triggering stimuli — the behaviour is triggered by specific stimuli.

Aggression in male sticklebacks

As hormone levels rise in the mating season, the male stickleback stakes out his territory, in preparation for nest building, and turns red. The red colour acts as an IRM triggering aggressive behaviour in other males. This can be tested by presenting dummy fish painted in different colours. Red males will only attack a model of a red colour. The male stickleback adopts a vertical position and displays his spines. The male defending his territory usually remains within its borders, attacking up to the boundary and then retreating again. If the opponent fish enters the territory the defending fish becomes more aggressive. Tinbergen also found that if a 'dummy fish' had a brighter red underside than a real invading male, the territorial male stickleback fought the 'dummy' more violently than the real invading male.

> **Knowledge check 35**
>
> Explain what is meant by fixed action pattern behaviour.

Mating and aggression

Animals fight for the right to reproduce and for social supremacy. An example of fighting for social and sexual supremacy is the so-called pecking order among chickens. Every time a group of chickens live together they establish a pecking order. In these groups, one chicken dominates the others and can peck without being pecked. A second chicken can peck all the others except the first, and so on. Higher-level chickens are easily distinguished as opposed to lower-level chickens. While the pecking order is being established, frequent and violent fights can happen, but once established, it is broken only when other individuals enter the group.

Some psychologists suggest there are innate releasing mechanisms in humans, for example:

- reflex behaviours like sucking
- babies smiling — elicit play from mother
- babies crying — elicit care from mother

> ### Evaluation
>
> - If human behaviour was made of fixed action patterns it would be rigid and inefficient, reducing the probability of survival, so the ability to change behaviour based on experience is important.
> - If human aggression is defined as 'any form of intentional behaviour directed toward the goal of harming or injuring another', as evidenced by the wide range of emotional, verbal and physically aggressive behaviours, it is difficult to argue that human aggression is fixed action pattern behaviour.

Evolution of human aggression

Evolutionary psychologists argue that the reproductive challenges faced by our ancestors can explain aggressive behaviour. For example, a man can never be certain that he is the biological father of his children unless he prevents his female partner having relationships with other men. This might explain why male sexual jealousy is often cited as a cause of aggression and domestic violence.

Aggression: infidelity and jealousy

Daly and Wilson (1988) propose that men have evolved different strategies to deter their partners from committing adultery, ranging from vigilance (e.g. watching their every move) to violence, and that these strategies are the result of male jealousy and paternal uncertainty.

If a man's female partner is unfaithful and has a relationship with another man, he runs the risk of cuckoldry — he may unwittingly invest resources in rearing children that are not his own. Male sexual jealousy may therefore have evolved to prevent infidelity by women and reduce the risk of cuckoldry.

Buss (1988) argues that males have developed strategies for mate retention. These include **direct guarding**, that is restricting the movements of his female partner, and **negative inducements**, such as threats of violence to prevent the female partner 'straying'.

> **Exam tip**
>
> Determinism or free will? Be ready to apply this debate to ethological explanations for aggression.

Wilson et al. (1995) found support for the link between sexual jealousy, mate retention and violence. In a questionnaire, women who indicated that their partners were jealous were twice as likely to have experienced violence from their partners.

Shackleton et al. (2005) demonstrated the link between mate retention, jealousy and violence. They surveyed 461 men and 560 women who were all in heterosexual relationships. The men answered questions about their use of mate retention techniques, and the women were asked about their partners' use of mate retention techniques and how violent their male partners were. There was a positive correlation between men who used mate retention techniques of direct guarding and negative inducements and their use of violence. Men also tended to use emotional manipulation as a mate retention technique. There was also a positive correlation (in women) between those who had jealous partners and being the victims of violence.

Duntley and Buss (2005) propose that when a woman is unfaithful, not only does the man lose a partner, but another man also gains a partner and that by killing his partner the man prevents his competitor from gaining a reproductive advantage over him.

Aggression and murder

Murder is the most extreme form of aggression and the vast majority of murderers and their victims are men (Buss and Shackleford, 1997). A disproportionate percentage of male murderers and male victims are unemployed and unmarried. A study in Detroit found that 43% of victims and 41% of murderers were unemployed even though the population unemployment rates were only 11%. Also 73% of male murderers and 69% of male victims were unmarried. This suggests that a lack of resources (e.g. less money, poorer housing) and the inability to have a long-term relationship leads to increased social competition and men murdering men.

Aggression and social status

In our evolutionary past, loss of status could be harmful for survival and reproduction. Men kill men to defend their status in a peer group and even though status is largely irrelevant for survival nowadays, it is an evolved behaviour that is passed on genetically. A UK study into the psychology of gang violence (Harris, Turner, Garrett and Atkinson 2011) found that status and respect seemed to be an important need for most gang members and that the need for respect contributes to gang affiliation in several ways. First, the belief that 'if they are seen as being part of a gang or being associated with older gang members then they will be respected by their peers' and second, the peer system was seen as a context in which participants could earn respect from their peers. This was particularly likely to be the case when participants experienced living in an environment characterised by competition and conflict between gangs representing different territories.

Evaluation

- **Application**: research into sexual jealousy and violence suggests that mate retention techniques such as direct guarding and negative inducement can be the early signs of a violent man. This is useful because educating people in these danger signs can reduce the likelihood of women becoming victims of violence.

Knowledge check 36

Outline how evolutionary psychologists explain domestic violence.

Exam tip

Make sure you can suggest one advantage and one disadvantage of the evolutionary explanation for aggression.

- **Methodological issues**: surveys are a self-report method and therefore may not collect reliable and valid data. If a man is asked to complete a questionnaire asking how violent he is towards his partner, then it is most likely that he will distort the truth due to social desirability bias. Similarly, a woman may be less likely to accurately report her partner as abusive if she fears recriminations from him, or because acknowledging it could mean the end of her relationship with him.
- **Gender bias:** research into domestic violence and infidelity is gender biased. The evolutionary argument for infidelity states that it is something a man must prevent a woman from doing, and does not really acknowledge the fact that men may be just as unfaithful as women.
- **Nature-nurture debate:** evolutionary explanations argue that aggressive behaviour has evolved through gene selection and is therefore biological. If jealousy and murder are evolved genetic responses to female infidelity then we would expect all men to behave violently to women, but clearly they do not. There must be an alternative explanation to explain why many men do not behave violently and others do.
- **Anthropomorphism** is the attribution of human characteristics to non-human creatures such as animals. It depicts them as creatures with human motivation. Evolutionary theories of aggression tend to use human behaviour, such as jealousy, to explain the animal behaviour.
- **Biological determinism** suggests that aggressive behaviour is innate (instinctive) and is 'in our nature'.

Social psychology: explanations of aggression

The frustration-aggression hypothesis

The frustration-aggression hypothesis is a theory of aggression proposed by Dollard and Miller et al. in 1939 (the Yale group). The theory proposes that aggressive behaviour occurs when a person's efforts to attain a goal are frustrated.

There were two hypotheses:

- Frustration leads to some form of aggression.
- Aggression is always the result of frustration.

The frustration-aggression theory has been studied since 1939, and there have been modifications. The revised frustration-aggression hypothesis (Berkowitz 1989) proposes that aggression is an externally elicited drive and suggests that frustration creates a readiness to respond in an aggressive manner but that aggression will only happen if environmental cues are present indicating that an aggressive response is appropriate. This theory suggests that certain environmental cues (e.g. guns) have become strongly associated with aggression and aggressive behaviour and that if a person becomes frustrated in the presence of these cues, he or she will behave more aggressively.

Knowledge check 37

Outline the original form of the frustration-aggression hypothesis.

Exam tip

Be prepared to give an example of an 'environmental cue to aggression' and to suggest how we learn to associate this cue with aggression.

Research evidence

Research into the aggressive cues hypothesis: Berkowitz (1967)

Participants were either angered or praised:

- No anger and frustration — the participant's work was evaluated positively by a confederate.
- Anger and frustration — the participant's work was criticised by a confederate and the participant received mild electric shocks and was thus both angered and frustrated.

The participants were then given the opportunity of delivering electric shocks to the confederate who had criticised their work and the angered subjects given more electric shocks.

Variation: Again, anger and frustration were caused by the participants' work being criticised by a confederate and them being given mild electric shocks:

- Condition 1: cues to aggression are present — a shotgun and revolver were present and the experimenter said 'these must belong to someone else doing an experiment in here'.
- Condition 2: no cues to aggression are present — a tennis racket was present.

Findings: The rate of electric shocks was higher in the aggressive cues (guns) condition. Berkowitz called this 'the aggressive cue' effect.

Dill and Anderson (1995)

Aim: To test Berkowitz's reformulation of the frustration-aggression hypothesis, looking at the effects of justified and unjustified frustration on aggression.

Procedure: Three groups of subjects all performed an origami (folding paper) task that was timed. The participant's success at the origami task was:

- blocked in an unjustified manner
- blocked in a justified manner
- not blocked at all

In each condition the experimenter stated that they would only present the instructions once and then start the timer. At a predetermined 'fold' in the origami task a confederate interrupted the experimenter and asked them to please slow down.

- In **the unjustified group** the experimenter responds, 'I cannot slow down — my girlfriend/boyfriend is picking me up after this and I do not want to make them wait.'
- In **the justified condition** the experimenter responds, 'I cannot slow down — my supervisor booked this room for another project afterwards and we must continue.'
- In **the control condition** the experimenter responds, 'Oh, okay I did not realise I was going too quickly, I will slow down.'

Afterwards the participants were asked to complete questionnaires on their levels of aggression and about the ability and likeability of the research staff. They were told that these questionnaires would determine if the research staff would be awarded financial aid, or would result in verbal reprimands.

Findings: The participants in the unjustified frustration group rated the research staff as having least ability and as least likeable, knowing this would affect their financial situation as graduate students. The justified frustration group rated the staff as less likeable and having less ability than the control group. The results support the hypothesis that frustration can lead to aggression.

Evaluation

- The theory is useful because it suggests that if, in society, we can prevent or reduce levels of frustration we can also prevent or reduce aggressive behaviour.
- Much of the evidence from laboratory experiments has low mundane realism, for example students being invited to give electric shocks — neither the sample nor the task are representative of day-to-day hassles.
- It ignores differences between people — not everyone who is 'frustrated' will behave aggressively, and the same person may respond differently from one day to the next.
- It is reductionist (environmental reductionism) as it suggests that aggression is simply an unthinking response to a stimulus such as a gun or knife.

> **Exam tip**
>
> Be ready to explain the difference between biological reductionism and environmental reductionism.

Social learning theory

In social learning theory Albert Bandura (1977) states that behaviour is learned from the environment through the process of observational learning. Bandura proposes that humans are active information processors who think about their behaviour and its consequences, and that children learn aggression by observing **role models** whom they then imitate. Children also learn about the consequences of aggression and observe whether there is **positive reinforcement** (through the model achieving what they wanted) or whether aggression is punished. This is known as direct or **vicarious reinforcement**.

According to Bandura, factors involving both the model and the learner can play a role in whether social learning is successful:

- **Attention:** if the model or the behaviour is interesting or 'stands out' the child is more likely to pay attention and learn the behaviour.
- **Retention:** the child needs to be able to remember and recall the information about the behaviour observed.
- **Reproduction:** the child needs to be capable of reproducing the behaviour.
- **Motivation:** the child needs to be motivated to imitate the observed behaviour. Reinforcement and punishment play an important role in motivation, as does vicarious reinforcement.

Bandura also found that children are more likely to attend to and imitate models they perceive as **similar to themselves** and thus are more likely to imitate behaviour modelled by people of the same sex. If a child imitates a model's behaviour and the consequences are rewarding, the child is likely to continue performing the behaviour. Bandura also proposes that children will imitate 'role models' with whom they identify. These may be people they know, such as parents or siblings, or fantasy characters or people in the media. The child identifies with a role model because the model has a quality which the child would like to possess. **Identification** occurs with the model and involves adopting the observed behaviours, values, beliefs and attitudes of the person.

Knowledge check 38

How does social learning involve cognitive factors?

Research evidence

Bandura, A., Ross, D. and Ross, S. (1961)

Aim: To find out whether aggression can be learned through imitation.

Procedures: Participants were children from a university nursery school (Stanford), 36 boys and 36 girls aged between 37 and 69 months (approximately 3 to 5 years). The mean age was 52 months (about 4½ years). There were two adult 'models', a male and a female, plus a female experimenter. Before the study began, the children were rated, using a 5-point scale, in terms of their physical aggression, verbal aggression, aggression towards inanimate objects and 'aggressive inhibition'. Each child had 4 marks which were then added together to give an aggression score.

The model (exposure to aggression)

Each child was taken on their own to a room where there were lots of toys including, in one corner, a 5-foot inflatable Bobo doll and a mallet. The experimenter invited the 'model' to join them and then left the room for about 10 minutes. There were three conditions (with 24 children in each):

- **Non-aggressive condition:** the model played with the toys in a quiet manner.
- **Aggressive condition:** the model spent the first minute playing quietly but then turned to the Bobo doll and spent the rest of the time being aggressive towards it, such as picking the doll up and striking it on the head with the mallet.
- **Control:** the children were not exposed to a role model.

Tests for imitation

The children were aroused (upset) by taking them into a room of attractive toys and then saying they could not play with these.

The children were then moved to another room which contained some aggressive toys (e.g. a mallet and a dart gun), some non-aggressive toys (e.g. dolls and farm animals) and a 3-foot Bobo doll.

The experimenter stayed with the child while he or she played for 20 minutes, during which time the child was observed through a one-way mirror. The observers recorded what the child was doing every 5 seconds, using the following measures:

- **Imitation of physical aggression:** any specific acts which were imitated.
- **Imitative verbal aggression:** any phrases which were imitated, such as 'POW'.

- **Imitative non-aggressive verbal responses:** such as 'He keeps coming back for more'.
- **Non-imitative physical and verbal aggression:** aggressive acts directed at toys other than Bobo, for example saying things not said by the model, or playing with the gun.

Findings: Children imitated the models they saw both in terms of specific acts and in general levels of their behaviour.

- **Imitation:** children in the aggressive condition imitated many of the model's physical and verbal behaviours, both aggressive and non-aggressive.
- **Non-imitative aggression:** the aggressive group displayed much more non-imitative aggression than the non-aggressive group.
- **Non-aggressive behaviour:** children in the non-aggression condition spent more time playing non-aggressively with dolls than children in the other groups.
- **Gender:** boys imitated more physical aggression than girls but not verbal aggression. There was evidence of a 'same-sex model effect' as boys were more aggressive if they watched a male rather than a female model and girls were more affected by a female model.

Conclusion: Bandura concluded that learning can take place in the absence of either classical or operant conditioning. The children imitated the model's behaviour in the *absence* of any rewards.

Knowledge check 39

Outline the three stages of the procedure in the Bandura study of learned aggression.

Research evidence

Brown and Ogden (2003) looked at the influence of parental modelling and control on children's eating attitudes and behaviour. Children aged between 9 and 13 were recruited from two junior schools and one secondary school in southern England. Children were approached by either the researcher or a teacher at the school and asked to give a consent form to their parents. It is estimated that about 260 children were asked for their consent and that 50% of children agreed to take part. Questionnaires were then given to 137 parents and children and 112 pairs of completed questionnaires were analysed.

The results indicated that:

- Both parents' and children's diets consisted of many unhealthy snack foods such as crisps, chocolate and biscuits.
- There was a strong association between a parent's and their child's snack food intake for all snacks in general, and for unhealthy snacks eaten the previous day.
- There were associations between parents' and their children's internal motivations and body dissatisfaction suggesting that modelling may have a role in the transmission of eating-related attitudes.

The research provides support for the modelling theory of parental influence and indicates that children's diets are affected by the types of food eaten by their parents. The researchers suggest that modelling appears to have a consistent impact and that a positive parental role model may be a better method for improving a child's diet than attempts at dietary control.

Evaluation

- This theory is useful because it suggests that if, in society, we reduce the amount of modelled aggressive behaviour we can also prevent or reduce aggressive behaviour.
- Much of the evidence is from laboratory experiments so has low mundane realism, for example the children being isolated and exposed to adults 'bashing Bobo' were put into a situation very different from everyday life. It is not clear that the children thought the 'aggression towards Bobo' was wrong and they may have thought the 'small Bobo' was a new toy.
- It is reductionist as it ignores all biological causes of aggressive behaviour.
- It can be criticised as 'soft determinism' because it suggests that children do not have the free will to make 'moral judgements' and that, if the conditions are right, any modelled behaviour will be learned.

Deindividuation

Deindividuation theory began as an explanation for why the behaviour of people in crowds is antisocial or violent. In contemporary social psychology, deindividuation refers to a diminishing of one's sense of individuality that co-occurs with behaviour disjointed from personal or social standards of conduct. For example, someone who is an anonymous member of a mob will be more likely to act violently towards a police officer than a person who is identifiable because he or she feels free to behave aggressively without fearing the consequences.

In his publication *The Crowd: A Study of the Popular Mind* (1895) Le Bon, a French psychologist, suggested that in a crowd, individual personalities become dominated by the collective mindset of the crowd. Le Bon theorised that in crowds, all suffer a loss of personal responsibility leading to an inclination, by the entire crowd, to behave antisocially. Le Bon was suggesting that deindividuation occurs when the individual becomes an anonymous member of a crowd and that as a result of deindividuation, the individual will behave in an antisocial manner and will fail to take responsibility for his or her actions. In sum, deindividuation is the loss of one's sense of identity, usually brought on by being an anonymous member of a group, or by hiding behind a uniform or a mask. This theory believes that the loss of one's identity leads to a lack of inhibitions and therefore to a change in normal standards of behaviour.

Research evidence

The Stanford prison experiment: Zimbardo (1971)

In this experiment 24 young, educated, male participants were assigned to the role of either a prisoner or prison guard in a mock prison. The study had to be stopped on day 6 because the guards lost their normal sense of identity and behaved appallingly towards the prisoners, humiliating them both emotionally and physically. All the participants had been tested for mental health prior to the experiment and no abnormal or aggressive traits were found prior to the study taking place. The guards wore uniforms and sunglasses and Zimbardo concluded that the guards' extreme and abusive behaviour was due to deindividuation. →

Exam tip

Make sure you can explain the meaning of deindividuation — and, if in an exam, you are given an example of a situation in which deindividuation could occur, make sure you can explain how this 'situation' may lead to deindividuation.

(For more details on the Stanford prison experiment look at www.lucifereffect.com.)

Rehm et al. (1987)

This study assigned either an orange uniform or no uniform to German school children who then played a football match together. Results found that the children who wore the orange uniform consistently played more aggressively than those who wore their normal clothes.

Diener, Fraser, Beaman and Kelem (1976)

In this research a woman placed a bowl of candy (sweets) in her living room for trick-or-treaters. An observer was placed out of sight in order to record the behaviours of the child trick-or-treaters. The observer recorded whether children came individually or in a group.

- In one condition, the woman asked the children identification questions such as where they lived, who their parents were, what their name was etc.
- In the other condition, children were completely anonymous.

In each condition, the woman invited the children in, and said she had to leave the room to look at something in the kitchen, but that each child should take only one piece of candy.

Findings:
- The anonymous group condition far outnumbered the other conditions in terms of how many times they took more than one piece of candy. In 60% of cases, the anonymous 'group' children took more than one piece, sometimes even the entire bowl of candy.
- The anonymous individual and the identified group condition tied for second, taking more than one piece of candy 20% of the time.
- The condition which broke the rule the least number of times was the identified individual condition, which took more than one piece of candy only in 10% of cases.

This suggests that being an anonymous member of a group does lead to antisocial behaviour.

Dodd, D. (1985)

This research evaluated the association between deindividuation and anonymity. Participants were asked what they would do, within the realm of reality, if their identity were kept anonymous and they would receive no repercussions. The responses were grouped into four categories: pro-social, antisocial, non-normative and neutral.

Findings: The most frequent responses were criminal acts and 36% of the responses were antisocial, 19% non-normative, 36% neutral and only 9% pro-social.

This study suggests that anonymity is an important factor in deindividuation. It also suggests that personality traits and characteristics are not a reliable predictor of a person's behaviour because in some situations behaviour changes from what would otherwise be the norm for a person.

Knowledge check 40

Explain why, according to Zimbardo, both prisoners and guards experienced deindividuation.

Institutional aggression in the context of prisons

Institutional aggression can be defined as the violent behaviour that exists within certain institutions and/or groups. Institutions may be entities such as schools or prisons, or large bodies such as the police or armed forces, or a whole society. In 2006, across England and Wales, there were 11,476 violent incidents between prisoners. This shows that prisons can be violent places for both prisoners and staff.

Two major models (theories) have been proposed in an attempt to understand why interpersonal violence occurs frequently in prisons: the dispositional explanation (the importation model) and the situational explanation (the deprivation model).

The dispositional explanation: the importation model

This explanation suggests that offenders enter prison with particular characteristics, such as personality traits, values and attitudes, and that these characteristics (dispositional factors) predict they are more likely to engage in interpersonal aggression. According to the dispositional theory, aggression is not a product of the institution but is caused by the characteristics of the individual.

Research evidence

Adams (1981) found that younger inmates are thought to have a more difficult time than older inmates when adjusting to prison life. As a result, they are more likely to have confrontations with other inmates and staff and view violence as appropriate during conflict.

Keller and Wang (2005) found that prison violence is more likely to occur in facilities that hold troublesome inmates. For example, prisons holding maximum-security inmates had higher levels of violence.

Harer and Steffensmeier (1996) analysed data from 58 male US prisons and found that black inmates displayed higher levels of violent behaviour compared to white inmates. They concluded that the black offenders often entered prison from impoverished communities with higher levels of violent crimes and so they bring into prison cultural norms which condone violence.

Poole and Regoli (1983) studied juvenile offenders in four different institutions, and found that pre-institutional violence was the best predictor of inmate aggression.

Evaluation

- McCorkle et al. (1995) claimed that the model fails to provide suggestions for how best to manage violent behaviour or how to reduce it in general.
- A limitation of the dispositional explanation is the suggestion that aggression is caused by nature rather than nurture, it ignores the environmental situation of the inmates and is thus a reductionist explanation.
- A limitation of research into institutional aggression within prisons is that there is a gender bias as it is only the behaviour of men which is analysed and therefore researchers take an androcentric (male-based) view of aggression.

Exam tip

Be able to define institutional aggression.

The situational explanation: the deprivation model

This explanation suggests that it is the situational factors of the prison that account for aggression and that the experience of imprisonment causes inmates stress and frustration, which leads to aggression and violence. For example, the overcrowding crisis in UK prisons forces many inmates to share cells, which is linked to an increase in interpersonal violence, self-harm and suicide. Harer and Steffensmeier (1996) suggest that an inmate's aggressive behaviour is a response to the problems and frustrations of adjusting to loss of freedom and to the isolation, boredom and loneliness of being in prison.

Research evidence

Zimbardo (1971) set up the Stanford prison experiment (see page 67 for details). Within 48 hours prisoners became anxious and depressed and Zimbardo suggested they suffered from deindividuation and learned helplessness. Zimbardo suggested that the students who played the role of guards became brutal and abusive towards the prisoners due to peer pressure, and that people are more likely to be aggressive when they dehumanise others in an institution without 'external restraint'.

Bandura et al. (1975) studied participants who were told they were working on a task with students from another school. In one condition, participants overheard an assistant refer to the students from the other school as 'animals', while in another condition they were referred to as 'nice'. When the participants were asked to deliver what they believed to be real electric shocks, higher shocks were delivered in the 'animals' condition. This provides support for Zimbardo's belief in the effect of dehumanising labels.

> **Knowledge check 41**
>
> What is the difference between the dispositional and the situational explanation of aggression in prisons or other institutions?

Evaluation

- Zimbardo's explanation of institutional aggression is useful as it has real-life relevance. Zimbardo (2007) claims that the same social psychological processes found in the Stanford prison experiment were also apparent during the abuse of Iraqi prisoners at Abu Ghraib prison in Iraq. These included deindividuation and dehumanisation which led to a lack of accountability for the brutal actions towards the 'prisoners'.
- However, McCorkle et al. (1995) suggest that the levels of stress associated with imprisonment are constant, whereas outbreaks of violence are not. They claim violence is due to the management of prisons. They studied 371 state prisons in the USA and found little evidence to support the connection between violence and environmental factors such as overcrowding and living conditions.
- Reicher and Haslam (2006) argue that institutional aggression in prisons is more to do with one group's way of thinking about the other group. For example, in the Second World War German captors treated their prisoners differently — British prisoners were considered equal and treated in a civilised manner, whereas Russian prisoners were seen as subhuman and treated barbarically.

- Research by both Zimbardo and Bandura is unethical and because all participants were students, the samples are not representative and cannot be generalised to the population of offenders in prisons.

Exam tip

Revise the issue of the interaction between nature and nurture, and be ready to explain why it is difficult to 'prove' whether the dispositional explanation explains aggressive behaviour in prisons.

Media influences on aggression

The question of how media violence might influence viewer aggression has been the subject of intense research for at least 50 years and studies have demonstrated an association between television viewing and subsequent aggression. Paik and Comstick (1994) suggest that when a child is exposed to aggression they behave more aggressively afterwards. In a meta-analysis of 217 studies that were carried out between 1957 and 1990, with an age range from 3 to 70 years of age, they found a significant relationship between watching television violence and aggression — the greatest effect was in preschool children, and more in males than females.

In longitudinal research, Huesmann and Eron et al. (starting in the 1980s) found that children who watched many hours of television violence when they were in elementary school tended to show higher levels of aggressive behaviour when they were teenagers. Also, Huesmann and Eron found that the children who had watched a lot of television violence when they were 8 years old were more likely to be arrested and prosecuted for criminal acts as adults. Interestingly, being aggressive as a child did not predict watching more violent television as a teenager which suggests that television watching could be a cause rather than a consequence of aggressive behaviour.

Knowledge check 42

If there is a correlation between watching television violence as a child and aggressive behaviour as an adult why can we not say that watching television violence causes adult aggression?

The effects of computer games

As many as 97% of adolescents aged 12–17 play video games on consoles such as the Wii, PlayStation and Xbox, or on portable devices such as Game Boys, smartphones and tablets. A survey in 2008 found that half of all teens who reported playing video games played every day, typically for an hour or more. Many of the most popular video games, such as 'Call of Duty' and 'Grand Theft Auto', are violent and several meta-analytic reviews have reported negative effects of exposure to violence in video games.

Research evidence

Anderson et al. (2010) concluded that 'the evidence strongly suggests that exposure to violent video games is a causal risk factor for increased aggressive behaviour, aggressive cognition, and aggressive affect and for decreased empathy and prosocial behaviour'.

However, Ferguson (2014) used data from the Entertainment Software Ratings Board (ESRB) to estimate the violent content of popular games from 1996 to 2011 and correlated this with data on youth violence during the same years. The study found a correlation between falling youth violence and the popularity of violent games. During the time period 'youth violence dropped precipitously despite maintaining very high levels of media violence in society with the introduction of video games'. Ferguson notes that 'the media narrative surrounding violent video games and youth violence may distract society from social concerns such as poverty, education and mental health'.

Huesmann and Moiser (1996) suggest three ways that exposure to media violence may lead to aggression in children:

- observational learning and imitation
- cognitive priming
- desensitisation

Observational learning

Children observe the behaviour of media models and may then imitate that behaviour, especially when the child admires or identifies themselves with the person on television. Television may also inform viewers of the positive and negative consequences of violent behaviour. The more real that children perceive violent televised scenes are, and the more they believe that they are like the characters, the more likely they are to try to copy the observed behaviour. Phillips (1983) examined crime statistics for the 10-day period following televised heavyweight boxing contests, and found a significant rise in the number of murders during that period.

Cognitive priming

Cognitive priming refers to the activation of existing aggressive thoughts and feelings. It explains why children observe one kind of aggressive behaviour on television but carry out a different aggressive act afterwards. The theory suggests that immediately after a violent programme has been viewed, the viewer is primed to respond aggressively because a network of aggressive memories are retrieved. Frequent exposure to violent scenes may cause children to store memories as cognitive scripts for aggressive behaviour which may be recalled in a later situation if it is at all similar to the original situation in which the aggressive behaviour was observed. In effect, the theory of cognitive priming is that aggression shown in media can trigger other aggressive thoughts and that after viewing a violent film, the viewer is 'primed' to respond aggressively.

Research evidence

Josephson (1987) demonstrated the importance of cognitive priming. In a study, a sample of 396 boys who were ice hockey players were split into two groups. Before a game, Group 1 watched a violent film and Group 2 watched a non-violent film. Impartial observers rated aggressiveness in the game. Those who saw the violent film behaved more aggressively (e.g. tripping and shoving other players).

Desensitisation (disinhibition)

This theory suggests that repeated exposure to violence in the media reduces the impact of the violence because people become 'desensitised' to the violence and they become 'used to it' (habituated) so it has less impact on them. This theory also suggests that people who watch a lot of violent television become less anxious about violence because they become used to it, so their emotional and physiological responses to violence decline. As a result they do not react to violence in the same way and they are more likely to engage in aggressive behaviour.

Exam tip
Revise social learning theory and the study by Bandura on page 65.

Exam tip
Be ready to write a sentence explaining what is meant by 'cognitive priming'.

Research evidence

Bushman (2009) supports this theory as participants who played a violent video game for 20 minutes took longer to respond to an injured person (stooge) than those playing non-violent games.

Knowledge check 43

Give one reason why children who play violent video games may behave more aggressively.

Evaluation

- The St Helena Study (a natural experiment). St Helena, an island in the South Atlantic Ocean, first got television in 1995 and contradicts many findings. Researchers concluded that very little changed in terms of antisocial behaviour. Most of the measures of pro- and antisocial behaviour either showed no difference or differences split between pro-social and antisocial behaviour. There were only two significant changes in antisocial behaviour scores and both scores were lower after the introduction of television.
- Research has usually focused on male-on-male violence, frequently done in artificial experiments using unrepresentative samples (e.g. male students).
- There are methodological problems to overcome, such as ethical issues, demand characteristics and, in laboratory experiments, a lack of ecological validity.
- Can we make valid statements about cause and effect from correlational and longitudinal research?

Aggression: glossary of terms

aggression (physical or verbal): behaviour that can result in physical and psychological harm to oneself, others or objects in the environment.

amygdala: an almond-shaped mass of nuclei involved in emotional responses that has been shown to be an area of the brain that causes aggression.

cognitive priming: the theory that immediately after a violent programme has been viewed, the viewer is primed to respond aggressively because a network of aggressive memories are retrieved.

deindividuation: the diminishing of one's sense of individuality and sense of responsibility that occurs when an individual becomes anonymous in a large crowd, along with behaviour disjointed from personal or social standards of conduct.

desensitisation: the theory that repeated exposure to violence in the media reduces the emotional impact of the violence because people become 'used to it' so it has less impact on them.

dispositional explanation of aggression: this suggests that offenders enter prison with particular characteristics that predict they are more likely to engage in interpersonal aggression.

environmental cue to aggression: the theory that environmental cues (e.g. guns) have become strongly associated with aggression and aggressive behaviour and that if a person becomes frustrated in the presence of these cues, he or she will behave more aggressively.

ethology: the study of animals in their natural environment. Ethologists are interested in how animal behaviours increase the animal's chance of survival and the reproduction of the species.

evolution of human aggression: the theory that the reproductive challenges faced by our ancestors can explain aggressive behaviour because a man can never be certain that he is the biological father of his children unless he prevents his female partner having relationships with other men.

fixed action pattern behaviour: instinctive and stereotyped behaviour that occurs in every member of a species in response to a specific stimulus called an innate releasing mechanism.

frustration-aggression hypothesis: the theory proposed by Dollard and Miller et al. in 1939 that aggressive behaviour occurs when a person's efforts to attain a goal are frustrated.

limbic system: a set of evolutionarily primitive brain structures located on top of the brainstem that are involved in many emotions such as fear, anger and aggression.

monoamine oxidase A: an enzyme (MAO-A) that is encoded by the MAO-A gene. Mutation in the MAO-A gene results in monoamine oxidase deficiency. A version of the MAO-A gene has been called the warrior gene.

serotonin: low levels of the neurotransmitter serotonin appear to be linked with aggressive behaviour.

situational explanation of aggression: this suggests that situational (environmental) factors in institutions such as prison cause inmates stress and frustration, which leads to aggression and violence.

social learning theory: the theory that behaviour is learned from the environment through the process of observational learning and that children learn aggression by observing role models whom they then imitate.

Knowledge summary

You should be able to demonstrate knowledge and understanding of:

- neural and hormonal mechanisms in aggression, including the roles of the limbic system, serotonin and testosterone; genetic factors in aggression, including the MAO-A gene
- the ethological explanation of aggression, including reference to innate releasing mechanisms and fixed action patterns; evolutionary explanations of human aggression
- social psychological explanations of human aggression, including the frustration-aggression hypothesis, social learning theory as applied to human aggression and deindividuation
- institutional aggression in the context of prisons; dispositional and situational explanations
- media influences on aggression, including the effects of computer games; the role of desensitisation, disinhibition and cognitive priming

Questions & Answers

This section contains 16 questions — five on issues and debates in psychology, three on relationships, four on stress and four on aggression.

The section is structured as follows:

- sample questions in the style of the Paper 3 exam
- example student responses at grade A/B (student A), demonstrating thorough knowledge, good understanding and an ability to deal with the data presented in the question
- example student responses at grade C/D (student B), demonstrating strengths and weaknesses and the potential for improvement

Examiner comments

All example responses are followed by examiner comments, which are preceded by the icon **e**. Examiner comments may indicate where credit is due, strengths in the answer, areas for improvement, specific problems, common errors, lack of clarity, irrelevance, mistakes in the meaning of terms and/or misinterpretation of the question. Comments indicate how the answers might be marked in an exam. Some questions are also followed by a brief analysis of what to watch out for when answering them (shown by the icon **e**).

Exam format

If you are studying A-level psychology, you will take the **Paper 3: Issues and options in psychology** exam at the end of your 2-year course. The exam includes synoptic questions to allow you to demonstrate your ability to draw together your skill, knowledge and understanding from across the full course and for you to provide extended responses.

Paper 3 is a written 2-hour exam in which 96 marks are awarded, comprising 33.3% of the A-level. There are four sections in the exam, each section is awarded 24 marks:

- Section A: multiple-choice and short-answer questions
- Section B: **one topic** from **option 1**, short-answer questions, applied questions and extended writing
- Section C: **one topic** from **option 2**, short-answer questions, applied questions and extended writing
- Section D: **one topic** from **option 3**, short-answer questions, applied questions and extended writing

As well as the mandatory **issues and debates**, this guide contains questions on **relationships** from option 1, **stress** from option 2 and **aggression** from option 3.

Assessment objectives: AO1, AO2 and AO3 skills

Assessment objectives (AOs) are set by Ofqual and are the same across all A-level psychology specifications and all exam boards. The exams measure how you have achieved the assessment objectives outlined in the table below.

AO1	Demonstrate knowledge and understanding of scientific ideas, processes, techniques and procedures.
AO2	Apply knowledge and understanding of scientific ideas, processes, techniques and procedures in a theoretical context; in a practical context; when handling qualitative data and quantitative data.
AO3	Analyse, interpret and evaluate scientific information, ideas and evidence, including in relation to issues, to make judgements and reach conclusions and to develop and refine practical design and procedures.

AO1 questions

Identify OR **outline** OR **describe**...

AO2 questions

Evaluate social learning theory as an explanation of aggression.

AO1 + AO2 questions

Describe and **evaluate** any two theories of aggression.

AO1 + AO2 + AO3 questions

Outline and **evaluate** research into the effect of stress on the immune system.

Multiple-choice and short-answer questions

On Paper 3 there are multiple-choice and short-answer questions and you need to read these carefully. When answering multiple-choice questions it is important not to jump to conclusions because one of the options may be a 'distractor'. For multiple-choice questions there will be four or five suggested answers, and usually you will be asked to shade in the 'box' applicable to the answer you suggest. For example:

Which **one** of the following statements describes a deterministic view of behaviour?

A People behave differently from one situation to another.

B People learn their behaviour.

C People cannot choose their behaviour.

D People are responsible for their own actions.

Examples of multiple-choice and short-answer questions are included for each of the four topics. Answers are provided on page 98.

Effective examination performance

Read the question carefully because marks are awarded only for the specific requirements of the question *as it is set*. Do not waste valuable time answering a question that you wish had been set.

Make a brief plan before you start writing an extended answer. There is space on the exam paper for planning. A plan can be as simple as a list of points, but you must know what, and how much, you plan to write. Time management in exams is vital.

Sometimes a question asks you to outline something. You should practise doing this in order to develop the skill of précis. Be aware of the difference between AO1, AO2 and AO3 commands (injunctions). You will lose marks if you treat AO3 commands such as **evaluate** as an opportunity to write more descriptive (AO1) content. Read the question command carefully and note the relevant skill requirement in your question plan.

Marks are awarded **in bands** for:

- AO1: the amount of relevant material presented. Low marks are awarded for brief or inappropriate material and high marks for accurate and detailed material.
- AO2: the level and effectiveness of critical commentary. Low marks are awarded for superficial consideration of a restricted range of issues and high marks for a good range of ideas and specialist terms, and effective use of material addressing a broad range of issues.
- AO3: the extent to which the answer demonstrates a thorough understanding of methods by which psychologists conduct research, for analysis, interpretation, explanation and evaluation of research methodologies and investigative activities.

Issues and debates in psychology

Question 1 (multiple-choice and short-answer questions)

1.1 Which of the following approaches is most likely to be described as environmental determinism? (1 mark)

A Biological approach

B Behaviourist approach

C Cognitive approach

D Psychodynamic approach

1.2 A student psychologist recruited 100 male participants and asked them to complete a questionnaire on aggressive behaviour. As a result he suggested that British people are innately aggressive.

Which one of the following biases is not demonstrated by the student's research? (1 mark)

A Gender bias

B Androcentric bias

C Alpha bias

D Beta bias

1.3 Name two types of reductionism in psychology. (2 marks)

Question 2

Outline one problem associated with alpha bias, and one problem associated with beta bias in psychological research. (4 marks)

ⓔ Question injunction = outline. This question requires you to show AO1 skills. You need to demonstrate your understanding of alpha and beta bias. You are not expected to provide more than 3–4 minutes of writing.

Student A
In the case of alpha bias there is a misrepresentation of behaviour because researchers overestimate gender or cultural differences. In the case of beta bias there is a misrepresentation of behaviour because researchers underestimate gender or cultural differences.

ⓔ **4/4 marks awarded.** Student A gives an accurate, clear and coherent outline of both alpha and beta bias.

Student B
In the case of alpha bias there is a misrepresentation of behaviour because researchers overestimate gender or other differences. In the case of beta bias there is a misrepresentation of behaviour because researchers overestimate cultural differences.

ⓔ **2/4 marks awarded.** Student B gives an accurate answer for alpha bias, but an inaccurate answer for beta bias. This is a common mistake.

Question 3

Outline what psychologists mean by reductionism. (2 marks)

ⓔ Question injunction = outline. This question requires you to show AO1 skills. You need to give an accurate, clear and coherent outline of reductionism.

Student A

Reductionism means breaking down, and explaining complex behaviours as being caused by simplistic single factors, such as inherited genes, so that scientific hypotheses about the causes of behaviour are easier to test.

ⓔ **2/2 marks awarded.** This is a clear and accurate outline of reductionism.

Student B

Reductionism means explaining human behaviour as due to biological factors ignoring social and cognitive causes of behaviour.

ⓔ **0–1/2 marks awarded.** This is a partially accurate but incomplete outline of reductionism.

Question 4

Discuss the value of reductionist explanations in psychology. (6 marks)

ⓔ Question injunction = discuss. This question assesses both AO3 and AO2 skills. The key phrases in the question are:

- discuss
- the value of reductionist explanations

To gain AO3 marks you need to demonstrate your knowledge and be able to explain the advantages and disadvantages of reductionism. You could:

- refer to the issue of psychology as a science
- refer to the need to test hypotheses
- contrast reductionism with holism

Student A

Reductionism means explaining human behaviour in terms of single factor causes. If psychology is a science, reductionism is an advantage because as scientists, to identify causes of behaviour, psychologists need to reduce complex behaviour to separate simple parts so reductionism is a necessary part of understanding what causes human behaviour. ⓐ Also, reductionism is useful because it allows psychologists to identify independent variables and formulate testable hypotheses that can be proved. ⓑ However, simplistic reductionist explanations for behaviour may prevent research into the more complex causes of behaviour. ⓒ In contrast to reductionism, holism is the principle that complex human behaviour cannot be understood by looking at each separate part of the behaviour, and that reductionist explanations cannot explain the complexity of human behaviour. ⓓ

ⓔ **5/6 marks awarded.** The discussion is effective and clearly focused on the value of reductionism. The answer is coherent and well organised with effective use of terminology. ⓐ The student makes an accurate point here but it is slightly circular and could have been explained more clearly. ⓑ, ⓒ The student makes another accurate point and a counter-argument is explained clearly. ⓓ The student shows understanding by contrasting holism to reductionism.

> **Student B**
>
> Reductionism is an advantage to biological psychologists as they can look at individual biological factors, such as genes, neurons, brain structure or hormones that cause behaviour. ⓐ However, reductionism is a disadvantage because it ignores cognitive and social explanations for behaviour and assumes that behaviour is determined by biological causes. ⓑ Also, complex behaviour rarely has a single cause, and biologically reductionist explanations for behaviour may be misleading. ⓒ However, even if it is reductionist, to be scientific psychologists need to carry out experimental research looking at one factor at a time. ⓓ

ⓔ 3/6 marks awarded. The discussion is partly focused on the value of reductionism, but the student focuses on 'biological reductionism'. The answer is mostly clear and organised with appropriate use of terminology. ⓐ, ⓑ The student makes accurate points that are not clearly focused on the question 'as set'. ⓒ The student makes a third clear point but again refers to *biological* reductionism. ⓓ The student shows some understanding, but the link between experimental methods and reductionism could have been explained more fully.

Question 5

What is meant by the nature-nurture debate in psychology?   (2 marks)

> **Student A**
>
> The nature-nurture debate is an argument looking at the extent to which, on the nature side behaviour is caused by innate biological factors such as genes, and/or on the nurture side behaviour is caused by learning and experience.

ⓔ **2/2 marks awarded.** The answer is accurate and includes an outline of both the nature and nurture assumptions.

> **Student B**
>
> The nature-nurture debate is an argument looking at whether behaviour is caused by nature, e.g. genes, or nurture.

ⓔ 1/2 marks awarded. The answer is very brief and only gains 1 mark because of the inclusion of 'e.g. genes'.

Relationships

Question 1 (multiple-choice and short-answer questions)

1.1 Which one of the following sequences shows the correct order of Duck's
phases of relationship breakdown? (1 mark)

A Dyadic, intrapsychic, social, grave dressing

B Intrapsychic, dyadic, social, grave dressing

C Intrapsychic, social, dyadic, grave dressing

1.2 Which of the features listed below is **not** a feature of the investment model of
relationships? (1 mark)

A Investment

B Satisfaction

C Joint bank account

D Commitment

1.3 One theory of relationship formation is known as filter theory. Three stages
of filter are proposed:

- The **first filter stage** is the social and demographic variables, where we
  tend to pick people with a similar educational and economic background to us.
- The **third filter stage** is the complementarity of emotional needs, where
  we decide how well as two people we fit together as a couple.

Outline the missing second filter stage. (1 mark)

1.4 Social exchange theory assumes that relationships are based on 'exchanges'
in which each person seeks to maximise their rewards and minimise their costs.
Outline any two of the four stages in the development of a relationship. (2 marks)

1.5 Psychologists suggest that relationships that start over the internet
are more intimate than those which start in a face-to-face physical
communication because you are able to be your true self without the physical
gating features present in face-to-face encounters.
List three features that may act as gating features in face-to-face relationships. (3 marks)

Question 2

From the evolutionary perspective, explain why physical attractiveness may be
an important factor in interpersonal attraction. (4 marks)

ⓔ Question injunction = explain. This question requires you to show AO3 skills.
You need to give an accurate, clear and coherent explanation to earn full marks.

> **Student A**
>
> The evolutionary perspective suggests that mating behaviour is motivated by the
> drive to reproduce successfully (produce surviving offspring). ⓐ If this theory is
> correct then both females and males will seek fertile mates and will be attracted
> to partners who show signs of good reproductive potential, indicated by physical
> characteristics such as smooth skin, glossy hair, youth and healthiness. ⓑ

🅔 **4/4 marks awarded.** This is an accurate answer. 🅐, 🅑 The student accurately outlines the assumption of the evolutionary perspective, and relates this assumption to the relationship between physical attractiveness and reproductive potential.

> **Student B**
>
> The evolutionary perspective suggests that mating behaviour is motivated by the desire to produce offspring and so people will be attracted to young and healthy mates.

🅔 **1/4 marks awarded.** This is a partially correct answer that is a statement rather than an explanation. The student has not related the answer to the question of physical attractiveness.

Question 3

Discuss the extent to which psychologists can explain the breakdown of relationships.

(16 marks)

🅔 Question injunction = discuss. This question requires you to show AO3 skills. Marks are awarded in bands. The banded mark descriptors for this question are:

13–16 marks Knowledge of the psychology of relationship breakdown is accurate and generally well detailed. Discussion is thorough and effective. The answer is clear, coherent and focused. Specialist terminology is used effectively. Minor detail and/or expansion of argument is sometimes lacking.

9–12 marks Knowledge of the psychology of relationship breakdown is evident. There are occasional inaccuracies. Discussion is apparent and mostly effective. The answer is mostly clear and organised. Specialist terminology is mostly used effectively. It lacks focus in places.

5–8 marks Some knowledge of the psychology of relationship breakdown is present. The focus is mainly on description. Any discussion is only partly effective. The answer lacks clarity, accuracy and organisation in places. Specialist terminology is used inappropriately on occasions.

1–4 marks Knowledge of the psychology of relationship breakdown is limited. Discussion is limited, poorly focused or absent. The answer as a whole lacks clarity, has many inaccuracies and is poorly organised. Specialist terminology is either absent or inappropriately used.

> **Student A**
>
> Psychologists have proposed several theories or models of relationship breakdown. Duck suggests that there are four stages in relationship breakdown. In stage 1, one partner feels dissatisfied with the relationship but may not express this; in stage 2, the dissatisfaction is exposed, and the partners argue and negotiate; in stage 3, the social stage, partners inform friends and family and these may interfere and takes sides; finally, in stage 4, if the problems cannot be resolved the relationship is ended. 🅐

One of the strengths of this model is that it sounds plausible and realistic and can explain why a wide range of relationships break down, including family relationships, relationships between friends as well as love relationships. However, the model describes how relationships break down not the causes of relationship breakdown. Also, not all relationship breakdowns will follow these neat and tidy stages, and the model focuses on what people do during relationship breakdown rather than on how they feel. b

An alternative explanation of relationship breakdown is proposed by Sternberg. He proposes that each of us has cognitive models, or schema, of our ideal relationship, which he described as a triangle comprising the three components, passion, intimacy and companionship. Sternberg proposes that when each partner in a love relationship has a similar requirement for the amount of passion, intimacy and companionship, the relationship will be maintained but when differences develop in the requirement for one or more of these components the relationship will break down. c One of the strengths of the Sternberg theory is that it sounds realistic, as passion, intimacy and companionship are three important components of love relationships. However, this cognitive model ignores the social context of a relationship, for example the wider circle of children, family and friends whose behaviour may also have an effect on the quality of the relationship. Also, while this model may be useful to relationship counsellors who can apply it to reveal differences between partners' relationship requirements, it is limited as it can only be applied to explain why relationships such as marriages break down. d

Yet another explanation for why relationships break down is proposed by behavioural psychologists who suggest that relationships are learned, and will be maintained, as long as each person in the relationship receives adequate pleasure by reinforcement. e Behavioural explanations of relationships focus on the idea that behaviour that brings about pleasurable consequences will be repeated, but this explanation is reductionist as it reduces relationships to packages of stimulus and response behaviours, ignoring the complex emotions and cognitive processes that may also be involved in relationship breakdown. f

Perhaps the biggest challenge for psychologists who study relationship breakdown is how to gather valid data on such a complex topic. Relationship breakdown is a sensitive topic, and ethical issues arise when using self-report methods to question people about relationship breakdown. Also, the validity of research into relationship breakdown may be low as asking people questions about the quality of their relationships may lead to social desirability bias, as people will try to make themselves 'look good' by justifying their own behaviour in a relationship. g Perhaps all we can conclude is that psychologists have explained some of the reasons why relationships break down, but that no psychologist can fully explain relationship breakdown. h

e **13–16/16 marks awarded.** This is a top band answer. The student has demonstrated good breadth of knowledge of research into relationship breakdown and the discussion is thorough and effective. The answer is clear, coherent, focused on the question and specialist terminology is used effectively.

[a], [b] The student outlines Duck's theory of relationship breakdown and then accurately and effectively evaluates the theory. [c], [d] The student outlines an alternative theory by Sternberg and follows this with a thoughtful evaluation. [e], [f] The student outlines the behaviourist approach to relationship breakdown and demonstrates understanding of the behaviourist theory in the evaluation argument. [g] The student demonstrates knowledge of research methods and shows understanding of the methodological problems facing psychologists who research relationship breakdown. [h] The student makes a final argument related to the question.

Student B

Psychologists have proposed several theories or models of relationship breakdown and Duck suggests that there are four stages in relationship breakdown. [a] One of the strengths of this model is that it can explain why a wide range of relationships break down, however the model describes how relationships break down, but not the causes of relationship breakdown. [b]

In contrast, Sternberg proposes that each of us has a cognitive model of our ideal relationship, which he described as a triangle comprising the three components, passion, intimacy and companionship. Sternberg proposes that when differences develop in the requirement for one or more of these components the relationship will break down. [c] However, this model is limited as it can only be applied to explain why relationships such as marriages break down. [d]

Behavioural psychologists propose that relationships are learned and maintained by reinforcement [e] but this explanation is reductionist as it reduces emotional relationships to packages of stimulus and response behaviours. [f]

Finally, relationship breakdown is a sensitive topic, and the validity of research into relationship breakdown may be low as asking people questions about the quality of their relationships may lead to social desirability bias, as people will almost certainly try to make themselves 'look good' by justifying their own behaviour. [g]

@ 6–7/16 marks awarded. Some knowledge of the psychology of relationship breakdown is evident but the focus is mainly on description and the evaluative discussion is only partly effective as the evaluation points are not explained fully.

[a], [b] There is little detail given of the Duck theory, and the evaluation could be argued more effectively. [c], [d] The student outlines an alternative theory by Sternberg but the evaluation point is not explained fully. [e], [f] Likewise, the outline and evaluation of the behaviourist approach to relationship breakdown is 'thin' and not fully explained. [g] The student shows some knowledge of research methods and understanding of the methodological problems facing psychologists who research relationship breakdown. Overall, the answer reads rather more like a list of evaluation points than a discussion.

Stress

Question 1 (multiple-choice and short-answer questions)

1.1 Which one of the following sequences shows the correct order of stages in Hans Selye's general adaptation syndrome (GAS) model of stress? (1 mark)

   A Resistance, alarm, exhaustion

   B Alarm, exhaustion, resistance

   C Exhaustion, alarm, resistance

   D Alarm, resistance, exhaustion

1.2 In the Holmes and Rahe research looking at the relationship between life changes and stress, what does the acronym SRRS stand for? (1 mark)

   A Stress Review Risk Score

   B Stress Rating Review Score

   C Social Stress Risk Scale

   D Social Readjustment Rating Scale

1.3 Kobasa (1979) found that some people deal with stress more effectively (the hardy personality). Two of the key traits of a hardy personality are (a) having a strong sense of personal control and (b) a strong sense of purpose and commitment. Briefly outline the 'third' trait of the hardy personality. (1 mark)

1.4 Which one of the following list is **not** an individual difference in coping with stress. (1 mark)

   A Type B personality

   B Responsibility at work

   C Type A personality

   D Locus of control

1.5 Psychological research has found that stress may reduce the effectiveness of the immune system. Briefly outline what is meant by the 'immune system'. (1 mark)

1.6 A local company is trying to help employees cope with stress so it decided to ask all its employees to complete a psychometric test. From the results shown in Figure 1, which employee is most likely to experience stress-related illness? (2 marks)

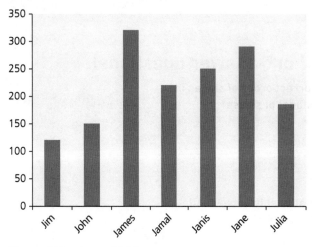

Figure 1 Employee SRRS stress scores

1 mark for correct identification of employee, and 1 mark for an accurate explanation.

1.7 What is the median SRRS stress score of the employees listed in Table 1?　(1 mark)

Table 1 Employee SRRS stress scores

Employee name	Jim	John	James	Jamal	Janis	Jane	Julia
SRRS stress score	120	150	320	220	250	290	185

Question 2

Dr Jones has two elderly patients who have ulcers on their legs. Ulcers are difficult to treat and over the past 2 weeks, both women have received the same treatment. In the case of Patient A, who always seems cheerful, the ulcers are responding to treatment and are improving, but in Patient B the ulcer shows little sign of improvement. He is worried about Patient B, who, having been recently widowed, seems to be depressed.

Using your knowledge of the role of stress in illness, explain why Patient B may be taking longer to heal.　(4 marks)

Question injunction = explain. This question requires you to show AO3 skills.

> **Student A**
>
> Kiecolt-Glaser found that long-term stress reduces the effectiveness of the immune system to heal wounds which may explain why Patient B is healing more slowly than Patient A. a Holmes and Rahe ranked loss of a partner as the most stressful life change and Patient B is stressed because of her recent bereavement. b So the difference in improvement of the ulcers may be explained by the indirect relationship between stress and illness — Patient B is more stressed than cheerful Patient A.

e **3–4/4 marks awarded.** Student A has written an accurate answer, demonstrating knowledge of the effects of stress on illness and has selected appropriate material to explain why Patient B is healing more slowly. The answer is coherent with effective use of terminology. **a**, **b** In the first sentence, accurate research is quoted and related to the source, and this is reinforced in the second sentence.

> **Student B**
>
> Patient B is more stressed than patient A and Kiecolt-Glaser found that stress reduces the effectiveness of the immune system to heal wounds.

e **1–2/4 marks.** Student B shows some knowledge of the effects of stress but the link to Patient B is not effective. The answer lacks detail and reads more like a statement than an explanation.

Question 3

You have been appointed as manager in a factory that employs 200 people. The factory makes plastic boxes and production is ongoing 24 hours a day, 7 days each week. The factory has a high level of sickness and absenteeism.

Suggest one change to factory procedures and explain why you think this change may reduce the levels of sickness and absence. (4 marks)

e Question injunction = suggest/explain. There are 2 AO1 marks available for an appropriate suggestion and 2 AO3 marks for a coherent explanation.

> **Student A**
>
> I would establish a free sports and social club for employees and encourage all employees to participate in clubs and social occasions. **a** Since the factory operates 24 hours a day, there will be employees on shift work and working night shifts which reduces the opportunity for workers to meet with family and friends. **b** Johnson and Hall found that workers who perceived their jobs to be demanding and who had low social support were at risk of developing cardiovascular disease, so the provision of a structure within which to develop networks of social support may reduce absenteeism caused by stress and ill health. **c**

e **3–4/4 marks awarded.** This is an accurate answer which demonstrates knowledge of the causes and effects of workplace stress. It is also coherent and uses appropriate terminology effectively. **a**, **b** In the first sentence, the suggestion is clear and detailed — knowledge is implied by the reason given for the suggestion in the second sentence. **c** This is made explicit and strengthened by quoting appropriate research and by explaining the probable effect of the suggestion in the final sentence.

Student B

Johnson and Hall found that demanding jobs that involved low levels of control were related to increased incidences of stress-related illness. ⓐ I would suggest that all employees be given some level of control over their workload and of which shifts they worked. ⓑ

ⓔ **2/4 marks awarded.** This is a brief but accurate answer, demonstrating some knowledge of the effects of workload and control. ⓐ In the first sentence, the explanation is clear but lacks detail. ⓑ In the second sentence, the suggestion is rather vague and there is no explanation given for the probable effects of the suggestion.

Question 4

Discuss the extent to which psychological approaches to stress management may be effective in reducing stress.

(16 marks)

ⓔ Question injunction = discuss. This question requires you to show AO3 skills. Marks are awarded in bands.

As supporting evidence, you could cite any or all of the following:

- Stress inoculation (Meichenbaum 1985), a cognitive behavioural therapy that prepares people to cope with stress before it becomes a problem.
- Increasing hardiness (Kobasa 1977), which encourages people to learn new ways to respond to stressors and teaches the behavioural, physiological and cognitive skills that enable them to perceive stressors as challenges.
- Geer and Maisel who concluded that people who have control in stressful situations are less likely to become stressed.
- Emotion-focused stress management: Lazarus and Folkman (1984) suggested that emotion-focused stress management helps people cope with stress.

The banded mark descriptors for this question are:

13–16 marks Knowledge of psychological approaches to stress management is accurate and generally well detailed. Discussion is thorough and effective. The answer is clear, coherent and focused. Specialist terminology is used effectively. Minor detail and/or expansion of argument is sometimes lacking.

9–12 marks Knowledge of psychological approaches to stress management is evident. There are occasional inaccuracies. Discussion is apparent and mostly effective. The answer is mostly clear and organised. Specialist terminology is mostly used effectively. It lacks focus in places.

5–8 marks Some knowledge of psychological approaches to stress management is present. The focus is mainly on description. Any discussion is only partly effective. The answer lacks clarity, accuracy and organisation in places. Specialist terminology is used inappropriately on occasions.

1–4 marks Knowledge of psychological approaches to stress management is limited. Discussion is limited, poorly focused or absent. The answer as a whole lacks clarity, has many inaccuracies and is poorly organised. Specialist terminology is either absent or used inappropriately.

Student A

Psychological approaches to stress management help people cope with stress by changing the way they think and behave when stressed, rather than by treating the physiological symptoms of stress. **a** For example, stress inoculation (Meichenbaum) is a cognitive behavioural therapy that prepares people to cope with stress before it becomes a problem. **b** An alternative psychological approach is increasing hardiness (Kobasa), which encourages people to learn new ways to respond to stressors and teaches the behavioural and cognitive skills that enable them to perceive stressors as challenges rather than as threats. **c**

One major advantage of psychological approaches is that there are no harmful physiological side-effects as there are from anti-anxiety drugs and beta blockers. **d** Another advantage of psychological approaches is that they are effective for both short- and long-term stress and can be combined with drug treatments. **e** For example, if people are showing extreme physiological signs of stress, immediate drug treatment may be needed to reduce physiological anxiety and to prepare people for interaction with a therapist. **f**

Psychological therapies, such as stress inoculation, are more effective than drug treatment, because if the therapy is effective, the cause of stress is removed, but with physiological treatments when the patient stops taking drugs the stressor remains and the symptoms of stress return. **g**

However, individual differences, such as personality traits, may influence whether psychological therapies are effective. For example, Kobasa would argue that psychological approaches may only be successful with patients who have a hardy personality because they have an internal locus of control and will be able to make the commitment to stick to the treatment to help themselves, whereas the time-pressured Type A personality might find the thought of setting aside hours of time to work with a therapist an added stressor. **h** Thus psychological therapies such as stress inoculation may only be effective with a biased sample of stressed patients, and they may not be effective in elderly people, or children, or those who find it difficult to express their thoughts and feelings in words. **i** Also, whether a psychological approach is effective may depend on the cause of stress, because stress inoculation and/or increasing hardiness would be neither ethical to suggest, or effective treatment, for someone who is stressed because of bereavement. **j** However, that said, for some patients, psychological approaches are very effective because once the treatment is complete, if patients continue to use the coping skills they have developed they will be more able to cope with other stressors in the future. **k**

ⓔ 13–16/16 marks awarded. This a top band answer. The student has demonstrated breadth of knowledge of psychological approaches to stress management and the discussion is thorough and effective. The answer is clear, coherent, focused on the question and specialist terminology is used effectively.

a–c The student briefly but accurately outlines the difference between physiological and psychological approaches to stress management and accurately outlines two examples of the psychological approach.

d–g The student argues an advantage of psychological approaches and gains marks by a well argued and coherent comparison with physiological treatments.

h, i The student demonstrates understanding by explaining, supported by evidence, a disadvantage of psychological approaches. **j** The student makes an excellent point about the effectiveness of psychological approaches depending on the cause of stress, and **k** concludes with a final argument related to the question.

Student B

Stress inoculation is a psychological approach to stress management and is cognitive behavioural therapy that prepares people to cope with stress before it becomes a problem. Stress inoculation involves three stages:

- Conceptualisation in which patients are encouraged to imagine stressful situations, analysing what is stressful about them and how they might deal with them.
- Skill acquisition and rehearsal in which patients practise specific skills, such as positive thinking, communication skills and time management.
- Application and follow-through in which patients are helped to deal with progressively more threatening situations while applying their newly acquired skills. **a**

There are no physiological side-effects from stress inoculation, but, unlike drug treatment, the benefit of stress inoculation will not be immediate. **b**

Psychological approaches are effective because they focus on the cause of stress rather than the symptoms, which means that if the therapy is effective, the cause of stress is removed. **c**

Also, these methods can be effectively combined with other treatment methods, such as drug treatment. **d**

However, stress inoculation may only be successful with patients who are able to take the time and make the effort to help themselves. **e** Also, research into stress inoculation is based on mainly middle-class educated people and the treatment may not be effective with children or the elderly or with people who are unable to make the effort to help themselves. **f**

ⓔ 6–7/16 marks awarded. The student has demonstrated some knowledge of psychological approaches to stress management but the material is quite descriptive and the discussion points needed further argument. The weakness of the answer is that it reads as a description and evaluation of stress inoculation rather than being fully focused on the question of *psychological approaches*. Some specialist terminology is used effectively.

ⓐ The student describes stress inoculation accurately, but there is too much AO1 material.

ⓑ–ⓕ The student makes accurate evaluation points that read rather like a list and that could all have been expanded and explained more fully. Compare this with the way Student A argued the discussion points.

Aggression

Question 1

1.1 Which one of the following is not either a neural or a hormonal mechanism in aggression? (1 mark)

   A   Testosterone

   B   Serotonin

   C   Cortisol

   D   The amygdala

1.2 Which from the list below has the MAO-A gene also been called? (1 mark)

   A   The fighting gene

   B   The warrior gene

   C   The aggression gene

   D   The male gene

1.3 Briefly outline the function of the MAO-A gene. (2 marks)

1.4 Which one of the following list is **not** true of ethological explanations for aggression? (1 mark)

   A   They are instinctive.

   B   They are species specific.

   C   They are learned.

   D   They are adaptive.

1.5 Briefly outline one evolutionary explanation for male aggressive behaviour. (2 marks)

Question 2

Briefly outline and evaluate the findings of one research study into the 'aggressive cues' hypothesis. (4 marks)

ⓔ Question injunction = outline and evaluate. There are 2 AO1 marks for an accurate outline and 2 AO2 marks for clear and effective evaluation. You are not expected to write for more than 4 minutes.

> **Student A**
>
> Berkowitz researched the aggressive cues hypothesis in a laboratory experiment in which student participants were either praised or angered by being given electric shocks, after which they were given the opportunity of delivering electric shocks to the confederate. In condition 1, cues to aggression

such as a gun were present but in condition 2 no cues to aggression were present. The rate of electric shocks given to the confederate was higher in the aggressive cues (guns) condition. a

These research findings are useful because they suggest that if aggressive cues are removed then we can prevent or reduce aggressive behaviour. b

A strength of the findings is that the aggression was measured quantitatively so that statistical analysis and comparisons could be undertaken. However, the findings can only tell us how many electric shocks were given, we have no qualitative explanation as to whether the findings were in fact influenced by the presence of the gun. c

Also, this laboratory experiment has low mundane realism because the sample were all young students and being invited to give others electric shocks is not a task that is representative of everyday life. d

Also, the research findings are environmental reductionism, as they suggest that aggressive behaviour is simply an unthinking response to a stimulus such as a gun or knife. e

e **4/4 marks awarded.** This is a top band answer, but the student did not need to write so much for 4 marks. The findings are accurate and clear and the evaluation is clear and coherent.

a The outline of the Berkowitz findings is accurate and detailed.

b, c The student makes two well-explained evaluation points and at this stage should have stopped writing as full marks had been earned.

d, e The student makes two more valid points.

Student B

Berkowitz researched the aggressive cues hypothesis in a laboratory experiment. In condition 1, cues to aggression such as a gun were present but in condition 2 no cues to aggression were present. The rate of electric shocks given to the confederate was higher in the aggressive cues (guns) condition. a

A strength of the findings is that the aggression was measured quantitatively so that statistical analysis and comparisons between the conditions could be undertaken. However, the findings can only tell us how many electric shocks were given, we have no qualitative explanation as to whether the findings were in fact influenced by the presence of the aggressive cue (gun). b

e **2–3/4 marks awarded.** The findings are accurate and clear and the evaluation is clear and coherent. a The outline of the Berkowitz findings is accurate and detailed. b The student makes an effectively argued evaluation point.

Question 3

Head teachers to report parents to police and social services if they let their children play Grand Theft Auto or Call of Duty

In a letter sent to parents warning about children playing computer games Nantwich Education Partnership says 18+ games can expose children to too much violence and sex, and that allowing children to play games, such as Call of Duty, is 'neglectful' and puts them at risk.

Adapted from an article by Claire Carter for *Mail Online*, 29 March 2015 (www.tinyurl.com/pg9nhf8)

Explain how playing violent video games may cause aggressive behaviour in children. Support your explanation with psychological evidence.

(4 marks)

ⓔ Question injunction = explain. These are AO3 marks. You should demonstrate knowledge of social learning theory as applied to how children may learn from violent video games and should select research material appropriately to support your answer. You are not expected to write for more than 4 minutes.

Student A

One of the risks is that young children who play these violent video games will imitate the aggressive behaviour they see on the screen. ⓐ Social learning theorists propose that aggressive behaviour is learned through indirect experience, that when children observe the behaviour of others they create a mental image of the 'observed model' and imitate the learned behaviour at a later date. ⓑ Bandura found that children imitated the aggressive behaviour of adult role models and that when children observe models who are 'rewarded' for aggressive behaviour they are more likely to imitate the behaviour because of the vicarious reinforcement. ⓒ Since video game players are often rewarded for their 'kills' by extra game-time and/or extra points scored, the rewards may make it more likely that the violent behaviour will be learned and imitated. ⓓ

ⓔ **3–4/4 marks awarded.** This is a top band answer. The explanation is coherent and clear. Knowledge of social learning theory is accurate and the material is used appropriately to explain how children may learn aggression from playing violent video games. The answer is generally coherent with effective use of terminology.

ⓐ, ⓑ The student outlines the processes involved in social learning. ⓒ, ⓓ The student expands on the explanation by selecting Bandura's findings and contextualising the explanation to the question and source.

Student B

Social learning theorists propose that when children observe the behaviour of others they create a mental image of the 'observed model' and imitate the learned behaviour at a later date. ⓐ Bandura found that children imitated the aggressive behaviour of adult role models, and because video game players observe a lot of violence on the screen the children may imitate the aggressive behaviour they observe. ⓑ

ⓔ 2/4 marks awarded. Some knowledge of social learning theory is evident but the explanation lacks detail and the link to the source is not effective.

ⓐ The student very briefly outlines the processes involved in social learning.
ⓑ The student mentions Bandura and relates Bandura's findings ineffectively to the question and source.

Question 4

Outline and evaluate ethological and evolutionary explanations for aggression.   (16 marks)

ⓔ Question injunction = outline and evaluate. This question requires you to show AO1 and AO2 skills. Marks are awarded in bands.

The banded mark descriptors for this question are:

13–16 marks Knowledge of ethological and evolutionary explanations of aggression is accurate and generally well detailed. Evaluation is thorough and effective. The answer is clear, coherent and focused. Specialist terminology is used effectively. Minor detail and/or expansion of argument is sometimes lacking.

9–12 marks Knowledge of ethological and evolutionary explanations of aggression is evident. Evaluation is apparent and mostly effective. There are occasional inaccuracies. The answer is mostly clear and organised. Specialist terminology is mostly used effectively. It lacks focus on aggression in places.

5–8 marks Knowledge of ethological and evolutionary explanations of aggression is present. The focus is mainly on description. Any evaluation is only partly effective. The answer lacks clarity, accuracy and organisation in places. Specialist terminology is used inappropriately on occasions.

1–4 marks Knowledge of ethological and evolutionary explanations of aggression is limited. Evaluation is limited, poorly focused or absent. The answer as a whole lacks clarity, has many inaccuracies and is poorly organised. Specialist terminology is either absent or inappropriately used.

> **Student A**
>
> Ethologists propose that aggressive behaviour evolved because it is adaptive because the most aggressive animals control access to resources such as mates, food and territory. Ethological psychologists propose that much animal behaviour is not learned but is instinctive, species specific and stereotyped. Lorenz proposed that species specific external signals act as a 'releaser' of aggression. For example, in the mating season, the male stickleback stakes out his territory and turns red and the red colour acts as a trigger to aggressive behaviour in other red males. **ⓐ** Although Berkowitz found that students engaged in more aggressive behaviour when 'aggressive cues' such as guns were present, aggressive behaviour in human males must have more complex causes, and cannot be genetic because there are no fixed environmental stimuli to which every human male instinctively responds in the same way. **ⓑ**

Evolutionary psychologists argue that ancestral reproductive challenges explain aggressive behaviour. According to this theory, because a man can never be certain he is the biological father of his partner's children he must prevent her having relationships with other men. This explains why male sexual jealousy is often cited as a cause of domestic violence. According to Daly and Wilson men have evolved different strategies to deter their partners from infidelity, ranging from watching their every move to violence, and these behaviours are the result of male jealousy and paternal uncertainty. ⓒ Wilson et al. found support for the link between sexual jealousy, mate retention and violence. In a questionnaire, women who indicated that their partners were jealous and did not like them talking to other men were twice as likely to have experienced violence from their partners. ⓓ

However, if aggression and murder are evolved behaviours then we would expect individuals who are in similar situations to behave in the same way but they do not. If aggression is evolved through gene selection it has a biological cause, but in the case of domestic conflict, even when jealous, most men do not beat their partners. ⓔ Evolutionary explanations are reductionist and deterministic, proposing that aggression in males is unavoidable, and caused by nature rather than by nurture. ⓕ Also, because males differ in the extent to which they are aggressive there must be an alternative explanation, and social learning theorists argue that violent men have learned to be violent by observing aggressive role models. ⓖ

A problem with researching aggressive behaviour is that when research uses self-report methods there are problems with collecting valid data. If a man is asked to complete a questionnaire which asks how violent he is towards his partner he will probably distort the truth due to his desire to appear more socially desirable. Similarly, women often deny that their male partner acts aggressively. ⓗ Also, much ethological research is based on non-human animals, and this can be criticised as anthropomorphic, attributing human characteristics such as jealousy to non-human animals, and comparing complex, culturally determined beings to animals. ⓘ In addition, evolutionary explanations of aggression tend to focus on physical violence in males and rarely look at female aggression. If human aggression is defined as behaviour intended to harm another, there is a wide range of emotional, verbal and physically aggressive behaviours engaged in by females as well and it is unlikely that there is a single gene for aggressive behaviour. ⓙ

ⓔ **13–16/16 marks awarded.** This is a top band answer. It is clear, coherent, focused on the question and specialist terminology is used effectively. The student has demonstrated accurate knowledge of ethological and evolutionary explanations for aggression and the evaluation is thorough and effective.

ⓐ, ⓑ The student accurately outlines the ethological explanation for aggression, supports this by carefully selected evidence and ends the paragraph with an evaluation point.

[c], [d] The student outlines the evolutionary explanation for aggression, perhaps in too much detail, but the final point in this paragraph is evaluative though it could have been phrased more effectively.

[e]–[g] The student makes several evaluation points — individual differences, reductionism, determinism, nature vs nurture. These could have been expanded and argued more effectively, but the final point in this paragraph is effective and well argued.

[h] The student demonstrates understanding of methodology regarding the evaluation of the use of self-report methods, [i] the point about anthropomorphism is well explained and [j] the student concludes by referring to the androcentric nature of much research into aggressive behaviour.

Student B

Ethologists propose that aggressive behaviour evolved because the most aggressive animals control access to resources such as mates, food and territory. Ethological psychologists propose that much animal behaviour is not learned but is instinctive. Lorenz proposed that species specific external signals act as a 'releaser' of aggression. For example, in the mating season, the male stickleback stakes out his territory and turns red and the red colour acts as a trigger to aggressive behaviour in other red males. [a]

Evolutionary psychologists argue that because a man can never be certain he is the biological father of his partner's children he must prevent her having relationships with other men and that sexual jealousy is the cause of domestic violence. According to Daly and Wilson men have evolved different strategies to deter their partners from infidelity, ranging from watching their every move to violence, and these behaviours are the result of male paternal uncertainty. [b] Wilson et al. found support for the link between sexual jealousy, mate retention and violence. In a questionnaire, women who indicated that their partners were jealous and did not like them talking to other men were twice as likely to have experienced violence from their partners. [c]

However, if aggression and murder are evolved behaviours then we would expect individuals who are in similar situations to behave in the same way but they do not. If aggression is evolved through gene selection it has a biological cause, but in the case of domestic conflict, even when jealous, most men do not beat their partners. [d] Evolutionary explanations are reductionist and deterministic, proposing that aggression in males is unavoidable, and caused by nature rather than by nurture. [e] Also, because males differ in the extent to which they are aggressive there must be an alternative explanation, and social learning theorists argue that violent men have learned to be violent by observing aggressive role models. [f]

(e) **7–8–16/16 marks awarded.** The student demonstrates knowledge of ethological and evolutionary explanations for aggression and the evaluation is partially effective.

(a) The student accurately outlines the ethological explanation for aggression.

(b), (c) The student outlines the evolutionary explanation for aggression, perhaps in too much detail, and quotes evidence to support the theory.

(d), (e) The student makes several evaluation points — individual differences, reductionism, determinism, nature vs nurture — but these could have been expanded and argued more effectively. **(f)** The student could have made the comparison with social learning theory more effectively.

Multiple-choice and short-answer question answers

Issues and debates in psychology

1.1 The answer is B. Behaviourism involves stimulus-response learning and suggests that all behaviour is the result of interaction with stimuli in the environment.

1.2 The answer is D. Beta bias involves generalising from an ethnocentric sample to explain the behaviour of all cultures, but the student researcher only applied the results to British people.

1.3 Biological reductionism; environmental reductionism.

Relationships

1.1 The answer is B. Intrapsychic, dyadic, social, grave dressing.

1.2 The answer is C. Joint bank account.

1.3 The missing second filter stage is the **similarity of attitudes and values**, where people with different values, attitudes and interests from us are filtered out.

1.4 The four stages in social exchange theory of relationships are:

- The sampling stage in which the potential costs and rewards of a new relationship are considered.
- The bargaining stage in which partners receive and give rewards to test whether a relationship is worthwhile.
- The commitment stage in which relationship predictability increases.
- The institutionalisation stage in which patterns of rewards and costs are established for each partner.

1.5 Any three from: age; physical appearance; gender; ethnicity; class; clothing.

Stress

1.1 The answer is D. Alarm, resistance, exhaustion.

1.2 The answer is D. Social Readjustment Rating Scale.

1.3 The third trait of the hardy personality is the ability to see problems as challenges to be overcome rather than as threats/stressors.

1.4 The answer is B. Responsibility at work may be a cause of stress but is not an individual difference.

1.5 The immune system consists of cells in the bloodstream, especially white blood cells, that defend the body against bacteria, viruses and cancerous cells.

1.6 James is most likely to experience a stress-related illness because his score on the social readjustment rating scale is more than 300, and scores higher than 300 have been correlated with physical illness.

1.7 220 is the median stress score.

Aggression

1.1 The answer is C. Cortisol is a stress hormone.

1.2 The answer is B. The warrior gene.

1.3 The MAO-A gene encodes monoamine oxidase A (MAO-A), which is an enzyme that degrades amine neurotransmitters, such as dopamine, norepinephrine and serotonin — all of which influence feelings and emotions.

1.4 The answer is C. Ethological explanations do **not** propose that aggression is learned.

1.5 Evolutionary psychologists argue that a man can never be certain that he is the biological father of his children unless he prevents his female partner having relationships with other men and that male sexual jealousy is a cause of aggression and domestic violence.

An alternative answer might be: Evolutionary psychologists suggest that men kill men to defend their status in a peer group and even though status is largely irrelevant for survival nowadays, it is an evolved genetic behaviour.

Knowledge check answers

Issues and debates

1 Ethnocentrism is the effect that your own cultural perspective has on the way you perceive other cultures and people from other cultures.

2 Emic constructs are traits that are specific to one culture (e.g. monogamy in Western culture) but etic constructs are universal traits that are the same across cultures.

3 When alpha bias occurs, research tends to emphasise and over exaggerate differences between genders. When beta bias occurs, research tends to minimise or ignore differences between genders. Any research is beta biased if it is conducted with an all male, or all female, sample and then applied to both genders.

4 Biological determinism suggests that the cause of behaviour is inside the individual, for example genetic makeup or the biochemistry of the brain, but in environmental determinism the cause of behaviour is outside the individual, for example a stimulus that evokes reflex behaviour in classical conditioning.

5 The biological level of explanation, the basic processes level of explanation, the person level of explanation (individual differences) and the sociocultural level of explanation.

6 Research into eyewitness memory is nomothetic because the memory of a group (sample of students) is studied and then generalisations based on this sample are made to explain all human memory.

7 Examples include: research that could cause stress; research involving drug treatment; research into illegal activities; and research into sexual behaviour.

Relationships

8 Breadth of self-disclosure is the range of topics discussed by two people and depth of self-disclosure is the degree to which the information revealed is private or personal.

9 All the participants in the Walster et al. computer dance study were students so the sample is age biased. Young people at a dance who are not looking for long-term partners may rate attractiveness as more important than older people.

10 Filter theory. The first stage is the social and demographic variables where we tend to pick people with similar educational and economic background to us. The second stage is the similarity of attitudes and values, where people with different values and interests from us are filtered out. The third stage is the complementarity of emotional needs, where we decide how well as two people we fit together as a couple.

11 (1) The sampling stage when the potential costs and rewards of a new relationship are considered and compared with other relationships. (2) The bargaining stage in which partners receive and give rewards to test whether a deeper relationship is worthwhile. (3) The commitment stage in which relationship commitment increases because each partner knows how to 'get rewards' from the other and costs are reduced. (4) The institutionalisation stage in which patterns of rewards and costs are established for each partner.

12 It may be difficult to obtain a valid measure of the costs and benefits of a relationship because (a) asking people about the quality of their relationships will involve using self-report methods but participants may not want to disclose negative details of their relationships, (b) the costs and benefits of a relationship are qualitative rather than quantitative and qualitative data may be misinterpreted, (c) how a person feels about their relationship may vary from day to day so a snapshot self-report is unlikely to be a valid measure of the long-term value of a relationship.

13 In individualistic cultures people choose partners based on personal preferences, but in other cultures partner choice may be based on family ties or in 'arranged marriages'. Thus the idea that people in all cultures are calculating the 'fairness' of the costs and benefits of their relationships is likely to be an imposed etic.

14 Rusbult suggested that a person will maintain, and be committed to, a relationship if satisfaction with the relationship is high because his or her needs are met by the partner AND if they perceive the quality of possible alternative relationships as low AND if they have already invested a great deal (e.g. financial, family, time) in the relationship.

15 Stage 1 (intrapsychic phase): there is little outward show of dissatisfaction with the relationship but one partner may be inwardly re-evaluating the relationship in terms of the costs and benefits. Stage 2 (the dyadic phase): the dissatisfied person tells the other partner and there are arguments as to who is responsible for the relationship problem. Stage 3 (the social phase): partners inform friends and family about the problems in the relationship and these others may try to help or may take sides. Stage 4 (the grave dressing phase): both partners try to justify leaving the relationship and construct a representation of the failed relationship that does not present them in unfavourable terms.

16 Physical attractiveness is a factor that attracts us to others because from an evolutionary perspective, attractiveness and good skin and hair indicate breeding success. The matching hypothesis suggests that we are attracted to people whom we perceive to be similarly attractive to ourselves. However, in a virtual relationship in which individuals are physically anonymous, people cannot see what each other look like and thus may form relationships with those whom in 'real life' they would reject.

17 In personal interaction, gating features are the physical barriers that may arise between people such as appearance, age, clothing, race and class characteristics and these gating features may distract people from expression of their true self. In virtual relationships, especially those where individuals cannot see each other, these gating features do not exist.

18 The attachment theory of parasocial relationships is a psychodynamic explanation. It suggests that the origin of the tendency to form parasocial relationships lies in childhood relationships with the primary caregiver. This theory argues that people who are 'insecurely attached' have a tendency to create parasocial relationships with celebrities because parasocial relationships do not come with the threat of disappointment and breakup.

Stress

19 When we are stressed the sympathetic branch of the nervous system stimulates the adrenal gland to release adrenaline, noradrenaline and corticosteroids into the bloodstream. These physiological changes cause the fight or flight response symptoms such as increased heart rate and blood pressure and a dry mouth.

20 High cortisol levels reduce the effectiveness of the immune system and lower bone density. They also increase the risk of depression and mental illness.

21 When we are stressed, the ability of the immune system to protect us against antigens is reduced. This is called the immunosuppressive effect of stress. In the long term, increased levels of corticosteroids reduce the production of antibodies (natural killer cells) that help to protect against viruses.

22 Long-term stress can damage blood vessels because adrenaline and noradrenaline increase blood cholesterol levels, leading to blood clots and thickened arteries causing strokes or heart attacks. Also, increased levels of cortisol reduce the effectiveness of the immune system.

23 The participant completes a questionnaire (the SRRS) indicating which of 43 life events they have experienced. Each of the 43 events has a fixed number of 'points'. Thus it is possible to calculate the total number of life change (readjustment) points for the 12 months.

24 A life changing event is an event that causes us to make a major change in our lifestyle, for example getting married or starting a new job. A daily hassle is an event that is annoying and irritating such as being stuck in a traffic jam.

25 Jobs that are demanding but that involve low levels of control have been found to be related to increased incidences of heart disease.

26 Example answer: The SRRS may not be an appropriate scale on which to measure the stress of students and other young people because many of the 43 items relate to marriage, divorce, family problems or changes in employment.

27 Type B people are usually not time pressured and hence do not often become impatient, angry or irritable. They tend not to feel guilt about relaxing and they work calmly and smoothly. Thus their nervous system is less likely to stimulate the adrenal gland to release stress hormones into the bloodstream.

28 Type A people move rapidly, they try to do two or more things at one time, they are competitive, they are hard-driving, impatient and aggressive. They tend to be achievement-oriented.

29 Physiological methods of stress management change the way the body responds to stress by treatments that reduce the physical symptoms of stress (e.g. reducing blood pressure), whereas psychological methods help people cope by getting them to think about their problems in a different way.

30 Benzodiazepine drugs slow down the activity of the central nervous system (CNS) and reduce anxiety by enhancing the activity of a natural biochemical substance, GABA, which is the body's natural form of anxiety relief.

31 Drug treatments are fast acting; drug treatments do not require people to change their lifestyles.

32 The person is attached to a machine that monitors changes in heart rate and blood pressure and gives feedback. The person learns to control the symptoms of stress by deep breathing and muscle relaxation and thus slows down their heart rate making them feel more relaxed. While they do this the biofeedback from the machine acts like a reward and encourages the person to repeat the breathing techniques. The person learns to repeat the breathing techniques in stressful situations.

33 SIT involves three stages. (a) Conceptualisation in which patients are encouraged to imagine stressful situations and analyse what is stressful about them and how they might cope with them. (b) Skill acquisition and rehearsal in which patients practise how to relax, and how to respond to stressors differently. (c) Application and follow-through in which patients apply their new skills while being supported through progressively more stressful situations.

Aggression

34 MAO-A stands for monoamine oxidase A which is an enzyme that degrades amine neurotransmitters, such as dopamine, norepinephrine and serotonin. The enzyme is encoded by the MAO-A gene.

35 Fixed action pattern behaviours are instinctive, predictable behaviours that always happen in the same way and only in response to a specific signal known as an innate releasing mechanism. Fixed action pattern behaviours are not learned and the behaviour is seen in every member of the species.

36 According to evolutionary psychologists, because a man can never be certain that he is the biological father of his children he must prevent his female partner having relationships with other men. Fear of cuckoldry and sexual jealousy is therefore suggested as a cause of aggression and domestic violence.

37 The frustration-aggression hypothesis proposes that aggressive behaviour occurs when a person's efforts to attain a goal are frustrated and that frustration always leads to some form of aggression.

38 Social learning involves cognitive factors because to learn the behaviour the child must pay attention to the behaviour and attention is a cognitive behaviour. Also the child needs to be able to remember and recall the learned behaviour and memory is a cognitive behaviour.

39 In stage 1, each child was left in a room with either a non-aggressive role model who played quietly with the toys, or an aggressive role model who punched the Bobo doll and hit it with the mallet. In stage 2, the children were upset by showing them attractive toys which they were not allowed to play with. In stage 3, each child was observed for 20 minutes in a room which contained a 3-foot Bobo doll, some aggressive toys and some non-aggressive toys. The observers recorded imitation of physical aggression, imitative verbal aggression and aggressive behaviour that was not imitative.

40 In the Zimbardo study, the prisoners had to wear the same prison smock, had their hair hidden and were known by a number not a name, so they all looked the same and lost their sense of identity. The guards all wore military uniforms, dark glasses and badges with numbers on, so they all looked the same and became anonymous, or 'just one of the guards'.

41 The dispositional explanation suggests that offenders enter prison with characteristics that predict they are more likely to engage in aggression. However, the situational explanation suggests that the prison situation causes inmates stress and frustration, which leads to aggression.

42 Correlational analysis looks at the relationship between two variables, but factors which have not been studied could also be involved in the relationship, or, the correlation may be the result of chance. Even if there is a significant positive relationship between watching television violence and adult aggression we cannot say that one causes the other.

43 Children who play violent video games may behave more aggressively because they see violence so frequently they become 'desensitised' so become less anxious about violence in real life because they become habituated (used to it).

Index